Tammy

Koning
Eizenberg

Julie Eizenberg

Koning
Eizenberg

Buildings

Introduction William J. Mitchell

Essays by

Aaron Betsky

Julie Eizenberg

RIZZOLI
NEW YORK

First published in the United States of America in 1996 by
Rizzoli International Publications, Inc.
300 Park Avenue South, New York NY 10010

Library of Congress Cataloging-in-Publication Data
Mitchell, William J.
        Koning Eizenberg: buildings / introduction by William J. Mitchell; essays by
        Aaron Betsky and Julie Eizenberg.
        p.   cm.
        Includes bibliographical references.
        ISBN 0–8478–1943–4 (hardcover). — ISBN 0–8478–1944–2 (pbk.)
        1. Koning Eizenberg (Firm)   2. Architecture, Postmodern—
California, Southern.   I. Eizenberg, Julie.   II. Title.
NA737.K68B48   1996
720'.92'2—dc20   96–13261
                                  CIP

Designed by Carol Newsom, Looking, Los Angeles
Front jacket illustration: 31st Street House, Santa Monica, 1993
Frontispiece: Preliminary sketches, various projects
Back jacket illustration: Erenberg House, Santa Monica, 1995
Printed and bound in Hong Kong

Contents

This book is dedicated to our parents.

Acknowledgments

The Buildings

Hank and I have always collaborated. We did our undergraduate and graduate theses together. Then, as now, we are asked, Who does what? How do you analyze a synergy or, for that matter, account for the input of ideas from other talented architects who have worked with us – like Tim Andreas? Tim joined us eight years ago, straight out of Penn State, and over the years he has become an integral part of our design consciousness. We work together closely, get our sketches confused, argue, and credit ideas to one another as the mood takes us. We truly wish the arts would acknowledge collaborative work as do the sciences and give up the preoccupation with individual authorship.

Some clients expected architecture and some were surprised by what they could have. We are grateful to them all. A selection of their projects, some big and some small, follows.

The Book

Thanks to William J. Mitchell, an unsung mentor to many, luckily including us; to Aaron Betsky for his continuing support; and to both for their ease and ability with the written word; to Heidi Williams, our long-term office manager, who made sense of the many drafts and handed them to assistant editor Megan McFarland and senior editor David Morton at Rizzoli, who guided us patiently through this first monograph. Via an introduction from Anne Rieselbach (now with the Architectural League of New York), David Morton initiated one of the first articles on our buildings back in 1986. We have not forgotten this and are grateful to them both.

We thank all the photographers for their interpretation of the buildings, and in particular Grant Mudford and Tim Street-Porter who, as seen from the credits, have persevered with us through many shoots.

As expected, the design of this book is yet another collaboration, this time among Hank, Tim, me, and our graphic design colleague, Carol Newsom, of Looking. It is wonderful to work with someone so adept in the printed medium.

J. E.

Bound for Santa Monica Bay:
An Introduction to the Work of Koning Eizenberg

Dear Bill:
Don't believe everything you read...
Sincerely,
Julie

William J. Mitchell

That was the letter accompanying the pile of reprints and clippings I got from Hank Koning and Julie Eizenberg when I set to work on this essay. Nothing more!

Of course, I immediately recognized the Australian cultural tic of self-deprecation. We all do it. We can't help it. Direct some appreciative words our way (and the published record of the work of Koning Eizenberg is full of them) and we'll just look somewhere else and mumble something sarcastic.

But this was also characteristically terse advise on how to approach the work: forget the framing texts and confront the architectural production itself. For the projects of Koning Eizenberg are proudly pragmatic. At their best, they engage important and pressing issues, often under very difficult conditions and with despair-provoking budgets. They are backed by a clear theoretical position, all right, and they are smart and knowing in their formal qualities, but all of that is worn deceptively lightly – you could miss it if you were not alert to the work's nuances. This is a body of work that demands to be understood as a series of practical solutions to the real problems of real people trying to live with dignity and grace in the late-twentieth-century city. Judge it on those terms.

Look at the Simone Hotel, for example. It is on one of the scuzziest Skid Row streets in Los Angeles; if you somehow didn't notice the surroundings, the careful (but not too obtrusive) security at the front door would tell you all you needed to know about the neighborhood. This is a single room occupancy hotel – the first to be built in LA in decades. Inside, packed as tightly as possible, are four floors of tiny but decent, cheerful, airy bedrooms. If you have very little money and need a place to stay, this is a solution. The plan cleverly contrives to squeeze as many amenities as possible out of the least amount of space and budget. On a deep, tightly bounded urban site, natural light reaches everywhere in the building. Of necessity, the bathrooms are communal, but they are distributed carefully throughout the floors so that each one serves a small group of residents. There could not have been much room or budget for public space, and in this context it is not easy to create public space that is safe and easily maintained yet not uninvitingly institutional; but the architects successfully carved out a relaxed, spacious lounge at the entrance and another one overlooking the street on the fourth floor.

Look again. The inexpensive, dumb stucco box is painted a jaunty yellow – close enough to the color of its surroundings to fit in comfortably, but just sufficiently different to invite a second glance. The architectural language is straight LA vernacular – almost. At the main entrance and along the street facade at ground level (where it really matters), a very small portion of that very precious budget was used for some spiffy detailing. There are arched openings and light, elegant, suspended metal canopies. There is a truly magnificent, studded, deco-like, stainless steel door, and a sign that Raymond Chandler would have loved to describe. Above, with a quiet nod to Charles Moore, the simple cutout windows don't dispose themselves exactly as you might expect. All of this tells you that the residents are valued and respected and that unpretentious dwellings in low-rent neighborhoods deserve – and can have – as much architectural smarts, subtlety, and wit as big-budget fancy ones.

Now look at the Electric ArtBlock. It sits on one of those weird, neglected, leftover lots that nobody really knew what to do with – a narrow strip along Electric Avenue in Venice where the tracks of the old Red Car line used to be. The program (made possible at the time by a new Los Angeles city ordinance) was to provide twenty combined living and working spaces for artists. The idea was to keep the artists from being driven out of an increasingly gentrified part of town; there wasn't much money to spend, of course. Orientation was determined by the proportions of the 50-foot-by-360-foot lot; ground-floor garages were needed; and twenty units were quite a few to jam onto the site. Simple arithmetic dictated a very long, four-story block covering the entire buildable area – a massing nightmare on a site with a low-rise commercial strip on one side and cute, dinky houses on the other. The solution was to create a sympathetic rhythm of white stucco blocks, with set-back metal-and-glass inserts in between on the south facade, facing the houses across the street, and a simpler, flatter facade answering the commercial buildings to the north. Then, the commonsense logic of differentiating the two facades was carried through the project. On one side you get single-height spaces, and on the other, double-height. Big studio windows are on the north; small ones, facing the houses and the sun, are on the south. The showier materials and details face the street, while it is simpler around the back. Appropriate to a beach community, each unit gets both a sunny side and a shady side, with places to sit outside and cross-ventilation to catch the sea breezes.

To the casual glance, this project presents itself as an unostentatious continuation of West LA's stucco-dingbat urban texture. There is nothing wrong with that. But, when you look more carefully, your attention is rewarded again and again. Suddenly you realize that the architects have slyly slipped in the unmistakable image of a train parked where the Red Cars used to run. You also recognize the ghost of California modern architect Irving Gill's magical, sunlit white boxes – one of which is not far away. You can even discern a faint resemblance to Renaissance palaces, with basements (wire-meshed rather than rusticated, as appropriate for car garages), *piano nobile* (with pipe columns, in the local manner), and regularly fenestrated attic. And look closely at those attic windows; again, they don't do exactly what you would anticipate.

Where did this mix of inventive, against-the-odds problem solving and sneak-up-on-you, subversive, deadpan wit come from? You don't have to look too far to see that it is a deeply embedded Australian tradition – one that arose from the hardships of bush life and was celebrated in the tales of Henry Lawson, in Joseph Furphy's great, shambling novel *Such Is Life*, and in the jingling doggerel of folk hero Banjo Patterson. It is the ethos of a country that mystifies outsiders by describing, as in Patterson's best-known ballad, the crushing effort of lugging a swag on your back from job to distant job as "waltzing Matilda," and by celebrating the jolly swagman who resourcefully solves his provision problem by stealing a passing sheep, rather than the "po-faced" forces of established order that bring down retribution upon him. The sprawling, suburbanized, immigrant city of Melbourne, where Hank Koning and Julie Eizenberg grew up and studied architecture in the 1960s and 1970s, was far from the bush of jumbucks and billabongs – but Koning and Eizenberg have not forgotten those outback cultural roots. They are still what Australians recall when they want to fabricate a hero figure – a Mad Max, or a Crocodile Dundee.

After graduating from the University of Melbourne in 1978, Hank and Julie were in Los Angeles in a flash. They were doing what ambitious young Australian artists, writers, critics, scholars, filmmakers, and designers have always felt that they must do – leaving that isolated, sparsely populated land to connect to a wider world. (Some return. Some don't. The story plays itself out in different ways.) At UCLA they encountered Charles Moore. Too independent to become acolytes or mimics of his style, they nonetheless learned some formative lessons from Moore, that generous, populist, sybaritic spirit. They saw how he respected, cared about, and listened attentively to the inhabitants of the places that he made. They saw, as well, how his work emerged not from the prescriptions of abstract doctrine but from close engagement of the quirky complexities and richly suggestive messiness of everyday human experience. They noticed that, through intelligent opportunism and sheer skill in handling space and enclosure, he could work architectural miracles with the tightest of budgets and the simplest of means – sometimes little more than a few cheaply constructed stucco walls. And they learned that architecture could be simultaneously serious and fun.

UCLA around 1980 was also the hot spot for research on shape grammars – a newly developed

Hank Koning and Julie Eizenberg, Stiny House, 1981

formalism for capturing knowledge of how to put things together. George Stiny, a professor in the Graduate School of Architecture and Planning, had shown how the idea of a generative grammar – long established in linguistics and computer science – could be extended to two-dimensional and three-dimensional compositions. This gave precise technical meaning to the intuitive concepts of architectural vocabulary and syntax and, provocatively, allowed automatic generation of works, in particular of architectural styles. Hank and Julie engaged this theoretical project as a way of sharpening their understanding of how architectural languages worked and how these languages might be deployed in practice. Eventually, they produced a memorable joint thesis in which they successfully established a grammar for Frank Lloyd Wright's prairie houses, then used this grammar not only to regenerate the original Wright corpus but also to grind out a potentially endless stream of disconcertingly plausible fakes. They gravely presented some of these problematic productions, all beautifully drawn in convincingly Wrightian style. Some of the crankier traditionalists on the faculty were not amused.

When they graduated, they went right out and started a small practice in Santa Monica. They started a family, too. They struggled; they got tiny projects, then some larger ones; they taught at UCLA, Harvard, MIT – the usual. But there was always one difference. From the very beginning, they determinedly found ways to make thoughtful and intelligent architecture with the most modest of means, in the most quotidian of settings. That was opportunity and challenge enough; they did not need more.

That is the story of Koning Eizenberg. If you know the history of Los Angeles architecture, it will have a familiar ring. For the City of Angels, valley girls, and the LAPD has always formed much of its architectural culture from the offerings of immigrants and exiles – from the Spaniards and Native Americans who built the missions, to the mid-twentieth-century wave of Viennese, to the Toronto-born Frank Gehry. There is another layer to that culture now – an architectural counterpart to the sharp scent of transplanted Australian eucalyptus that sometimes, surprisingly, floats through the Californian night air.

That is how I see it.

But don't believe everything you read.

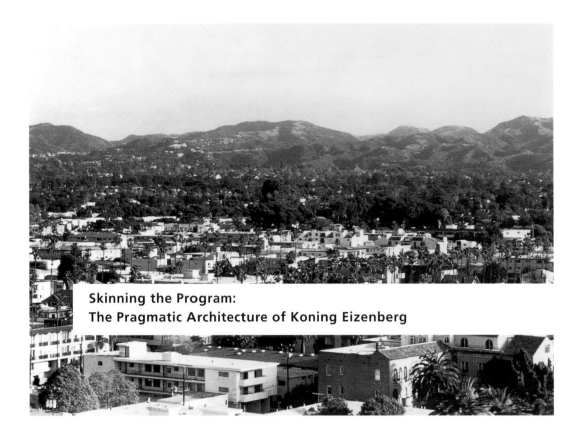

**Skinning the Program:
The Pragmatic Architecture of Koning Eizenberg**

Aaron Betsky

Hank Koning and Julie Eizenberg build. They also write, teach, and raise a family, but at the core of their existence seems to be a love of construction. Not the construction of sawdust and muscular structure, but the making of impure forms revealed in the Southern California sunlight.

The work of Koning and Eizenberg therefore represents a pragmatist approach to making building. That does not mean that they create boring, no-nonsense buildings that just work. After all, "There are many ways to skin a program," as Julie Eizenberg points out.[1] Some of this firm's skins are resplendent with bright colors, others arch into expressions of domesticity, leaving the constraints of program far behind. What they all share is an ability to transform the sedimentary layers of commonsense experience that make up the everyday reality of a city like Los Angeles into experimental forms that open up new spaces and new possibilities within that seemingly amorphous world.

Koning and Eizenberg's signal achievement has been to break through the division between a reliance on vernacular and a cult of invention. This split has long been expressed, on the one hand, in the modernist forms that architects have always

1 Conversation with the architect, September 16, 1995.

wished to impose on Los Angeles and, on the other, in the collage of historical elements with which the people who actually live in this place surround themselves. Instead of posing their buildings as alien interventions meant to show the way to a better world, or claiming that they are just embroidering on the existing fabric of the city, Koning and Eizenberg see their work as a clarification, crystallization, articulation, and strengthening of the forces and traditions – so vague, large, and abstract as to usually avoid clear description – that shape daily lives in Southern California.

The elements of their work derive from the local building traditions, in which wood (and lately metal) stud construction – that all-American technology – is covered with a flexible, colorful coat of stucco that can be pushed, pulled, and molded into a slightly expressive skin. Because of the particular sources of mythic narratives that generated the city of Los Angeles itself, this skin often appears to be a combination of Spanish colonial, English tudor, and streamline moderne styles that you can identify in the use of red tile, light and bright varied colors, only slightly sloped or curved roof shapes, and heavily decorated windows, doors, and other openings in otherwise unrelieved walls. Within this architectural fabric, the functional arrangement of spaces here, as in the rest of the country, is dictated by the need to create the maximum amount of private space while accommodating places for social interaction. Certain elements, such as the kitchen, serve as nodes where these two kinds of spaces come together. Peculiar to Southern California are the importance of the bathroom (which seems to derive from the worship of outdoor life and an obsession with the body) and the use of outdoor spaces as living environments.

In addition to such basic elements, small-scale construction in Los Angeles exhibits several specific traits. The most notable are the combination of bungalow and Spanish-colonial traditions in the making of gabled forms with expressive porches, entries, and chimneys that together compose the facade; and the so-called dingbat, a slab of living units that hovers over parking and storage areas. Finally, a reliance on planting to soften edges, hide aspects of security, and extend the romance of the Southern California idyll into outdoor space, creates a carpet of variegated shades of green that dominates the visual field in most residential areas. Civic, office, and apartment buildings often use a combination of these forms and organizational principles.

The parts and pieces mentioned above comprise a collection of architectural elements that could be organized in any number of ways, and which Koning and Eizenberg use to elaborate the already rich landscape of Los Angeles without either alienating the audience for architecture or merely restating the stiflingly obvious.

Indeed, something emerges that one might call style or signature, but which resides exactly in the act of interpretative composition.

This is what I mean by a pragmatic approach. The American philosopher and educator John Dewey called for a work of art that would integrate itself into everyday life, transforming our myriad actions and impulses into "an experience" whose concrete form and condensed evocation of this quotidian reality would make us aware of our world. This revelatory practice, embedded in concrete form, would make use of the rhythmic orders of composition to achieve its aim. Such a work of art would, moreover, remain tied to the necessity of building a "democracy," or participatory society, as its main function would be to allow viewers and users to understand their reality and thus be able to change it. According to Dewey, therefore, art was tied to both experience and education, as these would help people build a better world through the continuous exploration of the world they had already created.[2]

Over the last fifty years such a pragmatic approach to architecture has been practiced in various forms. Certainly Frank Lloyd Wright's organic architecture is an attempt to create a critical extension of the physical environment, using technology (what man can make) as a tool for letting loose a sense of wonder within the seemingly rational world, thus leading to the Deweyian "experience." As I have argued elsewhere, the work of such architects as James Gamble Rogers and William Wurster might also be seen in this light.[3] They experimented with readily available forms, used a methodology of combining these forms that most users or viewers would recognize, and strove to create coherent wholes out of disparate pieces, choreographing the parts of their constructions into richly layered environments that invited discovery.

What brings this work together is in fact its character as assemblage. This certainly does not mean that the work is an ad hoc gathering of preformed materials. These makers are, after all, still architects, not *bricoleurs*. Rather, one might see it as the modernization of an eighteenth-century typology in which the materials to be recombined according to a set of rules come from the existing landscape rather than from a classicist canon, and the rules are generated by the elements themselves. The role of the architect is – to use a musical analogy – to riff, pushing and pulling the materials (the rooms, the walls, the sequence of events) at hand to the point where they are transformed into something new which, because it does not shed its material sources, seems familiar.

2 John Dewey, *Art as Experience* (New York: Perigree Books, 1980 [1934]). See also Richard Hofstadter, *Social Darwinism in American Thought* (New York: George Braziller, 1959).
3 Aaron Betsky, *James Gamble Rogers and the Architecture of Pragmatism* (New York: The Architectural History Foundation, 1994). Architecture historian Gwendolyn Wright is currently working on a pragmatist interpretation of William Wurster and several other post-World War II "regionalist" architects.

The resulting constructions are thoroughly modern in the freedom of their combinatory solutions, their ephemeral nature as contingent pieces of function, and their frank use of mass-produced material. Yet they present an image of the world as seen through peculiarly rose- (or even bright red-) colored glasses. To have an experience, you have to experience material culture, translate it, and jazz it up.

This is the practice of Koning and Eizenberg. Through their teaching, research, and building, they have created a thoroughly pragmatic architecture. The question that remains addresses their compositional technique: What allows them to create their own particular strategy of pragmatic revelation? Where, in other words, does their style come from? Though this question might be essentially psychological, I think that their particular contribution has something to do with the imported foreign elements that invigorate the conditions under which they build. These influences are both literally foreign and, perhaps, idiosyncratic. They include practices they learned in Australia,[4] their love of such modern architects as Frank Lloyd Wright and, one might guess, the Dutch exponents of *de nieuwe zakelijkheid* (itself a form of pragmatism and usually expressed in German as *Neue Sachlichkeit*, "New Objectivity"), as well as their elaboration of the innovations of such local masters as Charles Moore and Frank Gehry.

Once in Los Angeles, Koning and Eizenberg entered a school still strongly influence by the work of Charles Moore. Moore was a pioneer in the reinterpretation of vernacular California forms. He had abstracted the basic Spanish colonial, bungalow, and Eastern shingle-style traditions into buildings that reveled in the very thinness of their skins and the flowing, unstable character of their interior spaces. Moore also showed that one could have fun with traditions, treating them as a scaffolding for one's own life. He developed his own language of architecture, one that included "saddlebags" for functional spaces, geometricized arches, serpentine circulation routes, and fragmented, sloped roof forms.

It was Frank Gehry, however, who came to dominate the architectural scene during the late 1970s and 1980s. "You can't help looking a little like Frank when you build here," says Eizenberg.[5] Certainly the firm's early work borrows heavily from Gehry's repertoire of form. For Koning and Eizenberg, this included the use of exposed stud construction and such materials as plywood, asphalt shingles, and concrete floors, as if they were undressing the normative buildings of the Los Angeles residential vernacular and revealing the pieces out of which these structures were made. Early

4 The influence of Australian building traditions is discussed by William Mitchell in his essay in this book, "Bound for Santa Monica Bay: An Introduction to the Work of Koning Eizenberg," p.8.
5 Conversation with the architect, September 16, 1995.

Koning Eizenberg works like the Hollywood Duplex of 1987, the Molloy House of 1987, and the California Avenue Duplex of 1984 also exhibit an interest in forms that slither away from what one might expect in a house by being just slightly larger, more skewed, and bulkier than "normal." If Moore had abstracted the articulating motifs, Gehry turned the forms themselves into more monumental, but also more ungainly, monoliths that, paradoxically, crumbled at their corners. Thus interior volumes began to bulge out and express their force without denying the traditional blandness of inward-turned domesticity that defined Southern California's residential landscape.

Using their interpretative composition, the playful decomposition of Charles Moore, and the expressive deconstruction of form they learned from Gehry, Koning and Eizenberg started to build up a practice of small houses and additions in the early 1980s. Though initially not very different from the work of such Gehry adherents as Frederick Fisher, it soon developed its own vocabulary. In the early houses, for example, there is a marked verticality, a play of cut-off geometries that at times recalls the work of James Stirling, and a rhythm of tight passages leading to loftlike living spaces. Their own house, completed in 1989, became a personal summation of this vocabulary. The dark-green front tower cants away from the "railroad car" of the main house to sit slightly apart from the residential grid. Its top becomes a glass turret, as if the solid form were undressing under the shelter of the roof. The seemingly idiosyncratic grid that covers this green block turns out to be the lattice for vines that have grown over the facade, making the house disappear into the lush vegetation of the neighborhood. You squeeze past this block, through a narrow doorway, and emerge into a large, multipurpose living room that mirrors itself in a lawn. Here the standard front lawn and the Spanish court become conflated into an extension of the house to the exterior.

What one notices most in these houses is their careful composition. Each door, window, and wall turns into a piece related to another in a compositional field. These compositions are essentially two-dimensional and become activated by the path one takes through the house. None of the elements in itself is exceptional, and most consist of standard hardware, off-the-shelf components, or simple constructions of wood and drywall. What makes them noticeable is a slight change of scale, their placement, and, above all, their relation to the other pieces in the room.

Koning and Eizenberg have become masters at rearranging the architectural pieces of Southern California domesticity. They could have remained elegant refiners of such domestic traditions, but their interest in social issues beyond the home has pushed them into another arena. Thus they have found ways of applying their de- and re-compositions at much larger scales, where the gestures have to be carried out in more abstract shapes. Starting with consulting work for the Fairfax Avenue neighborhood and the City of Santa Monica when they were barely out of UCLA, they have been trying to make forms that give coherence to the communal spaces in the "plains of Id"[6] that cover so much of Southern California.

6   See Reyner Banham, *Los Angeles: An Architecture of Four Ecologies* (New York: Penguin Books [Viking Penguin], 1973).

Koning and Eizenberg's 1987 low-income projects in Santa Monica are jewels of expressive practicality. The Fifth Street rental housing development reworks the basic principles of the dingbat, splitting it in two pieces that become residential towers and creating the beginning of a courtyard between these two densely packed forms. The Sixth Street project squeezes you past the front block to a more sheltered gathering place. In their Berkeley Street housing project, the dingbat starts to decompose into expressive elements slicing open the closed, white forms.

Each of these projects consists of simple, standardized spaces constructed out of readily available building materials and conforming to all applicable codes. What makes them come alive is their imaginative recombination of spaces; thus units of different sizes, intended for different income or age groups, are mixed. This compositional invention then becomes mirrored on facades that use equally standardized components to create lively patterns.

These buildings are considerably more abstract and modern in their appearance, as befits the mass housing (albeit at a small scale) we associate with the ephemerality and instability of modern living. The composition here becomes an act of stretching: codes are reinterpreted to allow the maximum amount of specificity and mixture of shapes, the budget is milked to accommodate such invention, and the skins extend into taut, white planes between these articulations. The forms are much cheaper to build than the heavier stucco blocks of market-rate housing, and Koning Eizenberg Architecture is masterful at making the best of such tight budgets. Even when designing an SRO hotel in downtown Los Angeles, they pulled apart the pieces of elemental domesticity to allow light, shared spaces, and an expressive, place-denoting facade to appear.

The expressiveness of the single-family house and the modernism of multiunit housing came together in the 1992 Venice ArtBlock, a collection of artists' lofts (mainly inhabited by screenwriters and lawyers who, in good Los Angeles fashion, dabble in the arts) that Koning Eizenberg designed on the site of a former Red Car rail line. The building has a trainlike appearance, as if the turret of which the firm is so fond had become the head of a long line of residential cars. Galvanized metal and other semi-industrial materials already present in this neighborhood join with wood and stucco to create a building that expresses its hybrid quality. Inside, the modernist loft finally becomes part of a repetitive residential module, and its method of construction remains present in the exposed structure.

Koning and Eizenberg until now have rarely strayed from their investigation of the residential components of Los Angeles, though they have created such brilliant institutional and commercial structures as the Ken Edwards Center in Santa Monica, the renovation of the Gilmore Bank in the Fairfax neighborhood, and a public gymnasium in the Sepulveda area of Los Angeles. Here again, the buildings work by a de- and then re-composition of existing elements. The Edwards Center quotes directly the nearby Santa Monica City Hall but also makes reference to Gehry's Santa Monica Place shopping mall across the street in its circulation, and then opens up a courtyard on top of a dingbat-like parking area. The Gilmore Bank project is no more or less than an elaboration and clarification of the forms of the existing bank. It introduces a larger scale, lets light into the space, and makes the building more accessible. Both of these projects create moments of great beauty in their window patterns and the sculptural assembly of stucco soffits, half-walls, and functional boxes. It is a beauty that remains embedded in the fabric of the buildings, yet opens them up to whole new categories of civic construction.

Recently, Koning and Eizenberg appear to be moving toward a more expressive style. This is especially true in their use of bright colors, such as the yellow ochre of the Tarzana House and the deep reds and blues of the Erenberg House in Santa Monica. These colors have always been present in the Los Angeles landscape, but they belong more to the terrain and the flora of the region than to its man-made traditions. Since both Koning and Eizenberg also admit to an ever-increasing interest in landscape (they briefly studied forestry), I wonder whether they are seeking to ground their work in a larger, more inclusive context, that of the geography and geology of Southern California. The recent work appears more abstract, airier, and more solid, as if it were seeking to become part of the landscape that may have existed before the sea of interpretative forms that now line the streets.

This brings up the basic dilemma Koning and Eizenberg face: How can they make forms that are pragmatically organic, monumental, and revelatory in a landscape dedicated to the erection of temporary signs or icons that allow one to navigate the continually changing tides of everyday life in Southern California? The beauty of their work depends to such a large degree on fixing compositions that stand still as one moves around them that you wonder how much expressive space they can claim. Moreover, because the work is part of the Southern California architecture tradition, they have found themselves restricted to that region for much of their building career.

These are restrictions and tensions that seem to animate the work of Hank Koning and Julie Eizenberg, producing continually changing compositions. As they build on these compositions, Koning and Eizenberg articulate what one critic calls "the dross" that shapes our daily landscape into moments of pure beauty and elegant poise.[7] Theirs is a pragmatic way to make moments of sense within the confusion of Los Angeles, for it reforms and represents our world to us, thereby ordering our experiences. There are indeed many ways to skin a program, but Koning and Eizenberg are especially good at programming their skins to reveal the specifics of daily life in a particular place of inherent beauty and with a verve that surpasses the logic of mere construction. Their work enters the realm of the active composition of common sense, order, and sensuality in the sprawl of our urban environment.

7 Lars Lerup, "Stim & Dross: Rethinking the Metropolis," *Assemblage 25* (December 1994); 82.

Buildings

Sepulveda Gym

In Mexico there is a tradition of buildings
and walls with perforated masonry skins. At
certain times of day sunlight squeezes through
the small openings, achieving a palpable density. This tradition inspired the design of the
gym and provided a framework for admitting
light inside a tough building type that is very
susceptible to vandalism. The gym serves a
low-income neighborhood and adds an indoor
basketball court and meeting rooms to existing
recreation facilities in a public park. Building in
many of LA's public parks is a balancing act
between the need to respond to real issues of
vandalism and security, and a desire to make
people-friendly spaces. We are eager to see
how this gymnasium fares. Together with the
city, we took big risks with maintenance and
security by including broad areas of
glazing and skylights.

East elevation

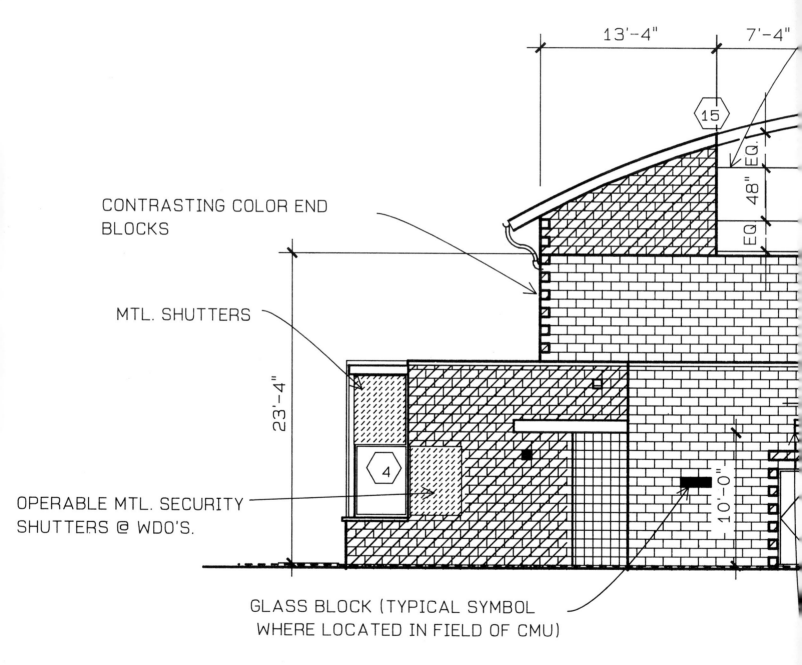

CONTRASTING COLOR END BLOCKS

MTL. SHUTTERS

OPERABLE MTL. SECURITY SHUTTERS @ WDO'S.

GLASS BLOCK (TYPICAL SYMBOL WHERE LOCATED IN FIELD OF CMU)

13'-4"

7'-4"

15

48" EQ.

EQ.

23'-4"

4

10'-0"

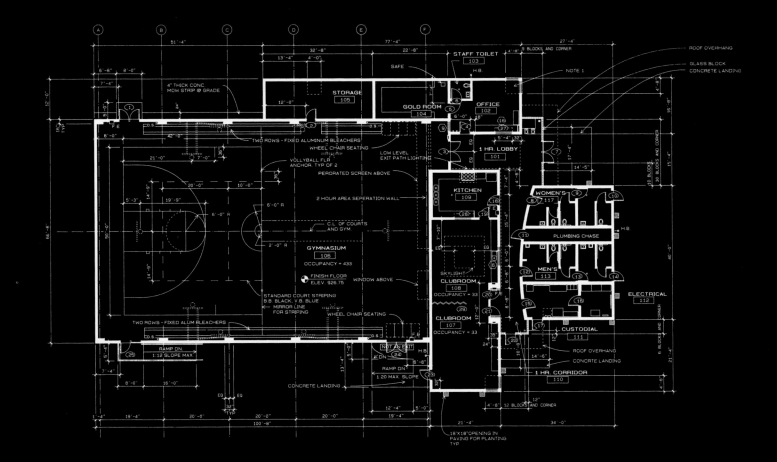

Floor plan

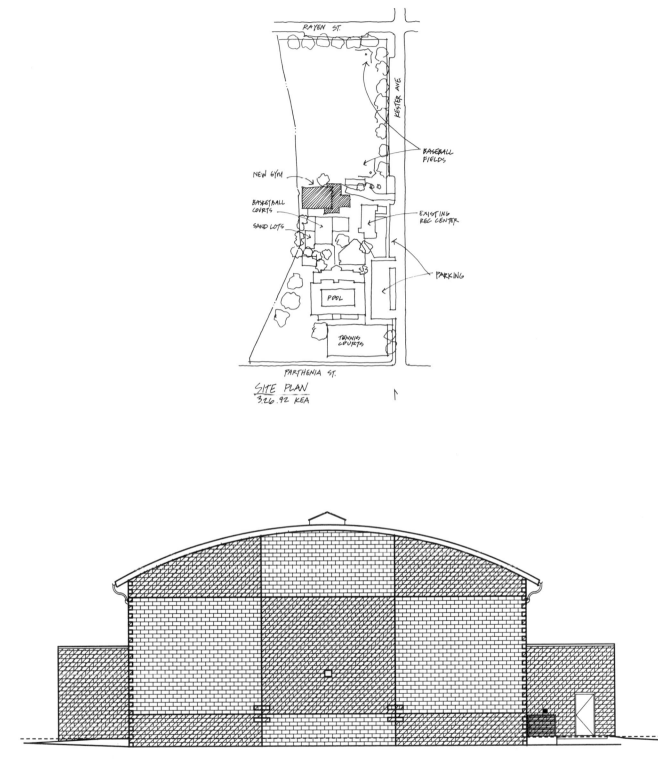

RAYEN ST.

KESTER AVE

BASEBALL
FIELDS

NEW GYM

BASKETBALL
COURTS

SAND LOTS

EXISTING
REC CENTER

PARKING

POOL

TENNIS
COURTS

PARTHENIA ST.

SITE PLAN
3.26.92 KEA

West elevation

Simone Hotel

The Simone was the first new single room occupancy (SRO) hotel built in LA in thirty years. Its name, in fact, is taken from one that had recently been demolished. SRO's are the first layer of permanent housing available to homeless or transient people – the first step off the street – although the typical resident may live in and out of SRO housing for his or her adult life. Although nonprofit organizations like the Skid Row Housing Trust (owner and client of the Simone) were remodeling existing SRO's, the chance to build a new one was seen as a great opportunity to explore their full potential.

Old SRO's recall scenes from hard-boiled detective movies: single rooms with lots of cigarette smoke, minimal furniture, and a bathroom down the hall. An SRO today is a safe haven providing the opportunity to socialize. The Simone has single rooms with bathrooms down the hall, but it also has community spaces and shared kitchens and laundries.

Many of the residents have had institutional experiences, and our client wanted a safe, non-threatening environment free from surveillance cameras. Budget prevented the use of air-conditioning. These two design requirements were worked together to an advantage: hallways have natural light and ventilation and views through to other spaces, enhancing security, comfort, and the overall relaxed sensibility that prevails in the hotel. Apart from the passive cooling, the most experimental element of the design was the big glass windows on the street, included as a deliberately street-friendly gesture. None of us, client or architect, was entirely sure they would survive, but they have.

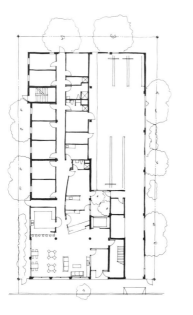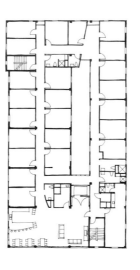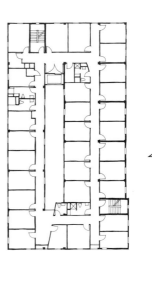

Ground floor plan

Fourth floor plan

Typical floor plan

0   15   30   60

South elevation

East elevation

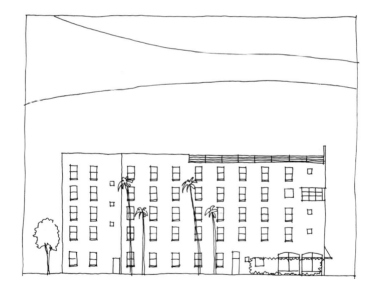

North elevation

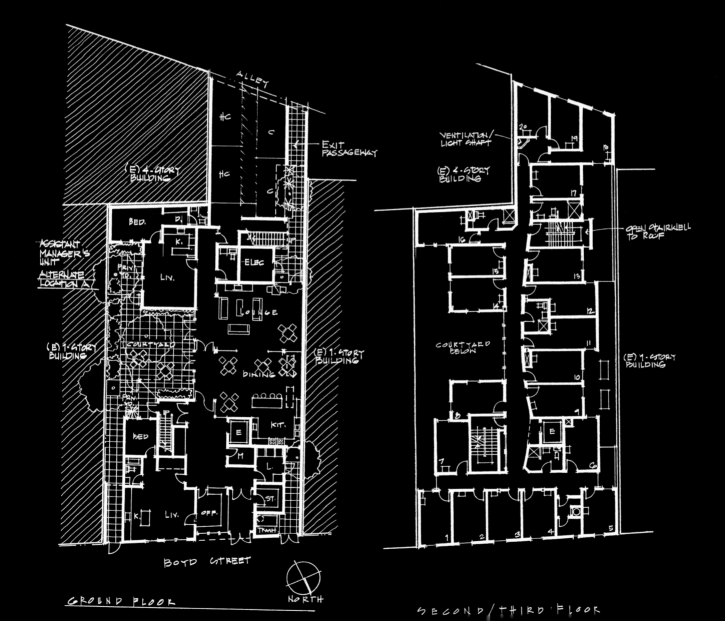

ALLEY

(E) 4·STORY
BUILDING

HC

HC

C

C

EXIT
PASSAGEWAY

ASSISTANT
MANAGER'S
UNIT
ALTERNATE
LOCATION A

BED.

D.

K.

PRIV.
TO.

LIV.

ELEC

LOUNGE

(E) 1·STORY
BUILDING

COURTYARD

DINING

(E) 1·STORY
BUILDING

PRIV.
TO.

BED

KIT.

E

M

L.

K.

LIV.

OFF.

ST.

TRASH

BOYD STREET

GROUND FLOOR

NORTH

VENTILATION/
LIGHT SHAFT

(E) 4·STORY
BUILDING

20

19

18

17

16

15

OPEN STAIRWELL
TO ROOF

14

13

12

COURTYARD
BELOW

11

10

(E) 1·STORY
BUILDING

8

9

E

7

6

C.

1

2

3

4

5

SECOND/THIRD FLOOR

Boyd Hotel

The Boyd Hotel is a new, 63-room, single room occupancy hotel located on the edge of the old toy district in downtown LA. It was developed for the nonprofit Skid Row Housing Trust and provides modest single rooms with shared bathrooms and communal facilites: kitchen, lounge, and laundry. The design drew on our experience with its sister project, the Simone Hotel, on Skid Row (p. 34). This time we were able to extend the sequence of communal spaces to include a tree-filled courtyard. The curvaceous entry and lobby ceiling evolved through experimentation with the plasticity of stucco and plaster construction in other projects. It is an exuberant gesture meant to enliven what is, due to budget, a restrained design.

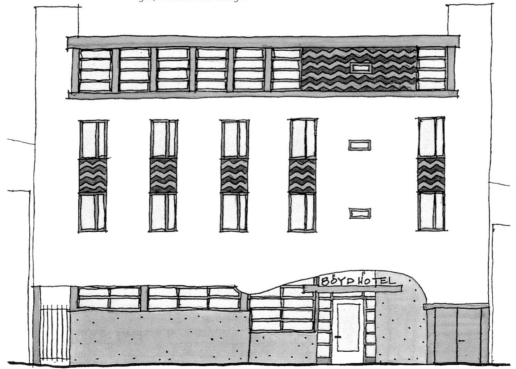

Preliminary sketches

Gilmore Bank

When the Gilmore Bank opened in 1955, the 10,000-square-foot building was essentially a vernacular warehouse structure cleverly clothed as a bank. Pictures of the bank when it first opened reveal its simplicity, openness, and elegance; yet it was a modest building. Forty years later and minimally altered, this combination of design sophistication and ease-of-use was still endearing to bank customers and local people. The bank had become a secret neighborhood landmark for longtime residents and new architecture cognoscenti. The building and the bank's image, however, were worn and needed refreshing. It was also time to update its operations, reduce its energy consumption, and bring the structure up to current code.

We blasted five giant skylights into the bank chamber, exposing the roof rafters and flooding the space with diffuse light; removed excessive exterior planting to increase visibility into the bank and add further light; added light shelves on the south and east to shade the glass and minimize sun penetration; replaced all glazing with energy-efficient double-glazed units that reduce heat gain and loss; and installed new, electronically controlled artificial lighting that automatically supplements daylight only when needed. In total, these combined strategies not only vitalize the bank's image but also halve the building's energy load.

We moved the president's office to the east, relocated the east entry, added a conference room, staircase, elevator, and basement rooms, and reconfigured the west entry. We designed a new teller line and removed the loan counter that ran continuously on the south side, replacing it with an open-plan loan platform with new furniture and carpeting. All furniture is new except the sit-down check writing table. Yet, walking into the bank, one is not quite sure what is old and what is new. The two layers of the bank are fused; many patrons now enjoy the heightened design sensibility, the light, the lack of pretension, and the game of weaving the old and the new.

49

Opening day, 1955

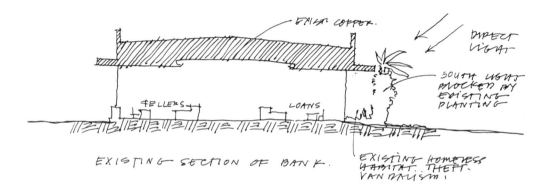

EXIST. COPPER.

DIRECT LIGHT

SOUTH LIGHT BLOCKED BY EXISTING PLANTING

TELLERS

LOANS

EXISTING SECTION OF BANK.

EXISTING HOMELESS HABITAT. THEFT. VANDALISM.

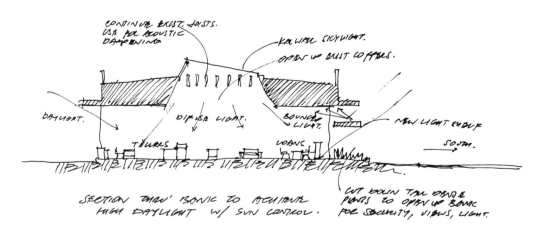

CONTINUE EXIST. JOISTS. USE FOR ACOUSTIC DAMPENING

NEW WALL SKYLIGHT.

OPEN UP EXIST COFFERS.

DAYLIGHT.

DIFFUSE LIGHT.

BOUNCE LIGHT.

NEW LIGHT SHELF.

TELLERS

LOANS

SOUTH.

SECTION THRU' BANK TO ACHIEVE HIGH DAYLIGHT W/ SUN CONTROL.

CUT DOWN TALL DENSE PLANTS TO OPEN UP BANK FOR SECURITY, VIEWS, LIGHT.

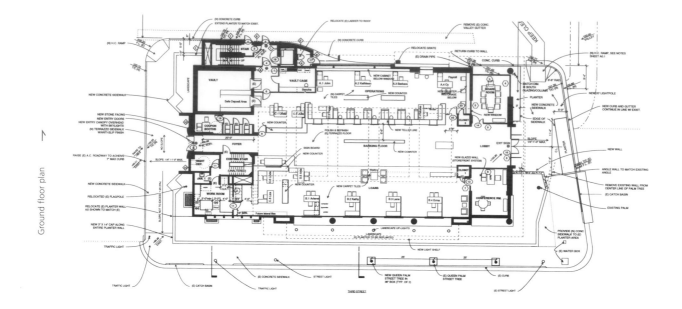

Ground floor plan

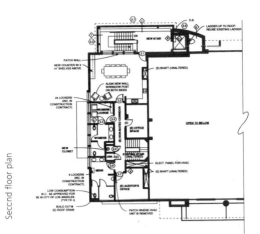

Second floor plan

New elevator tower and second floor access

New south face sun control

Opening day, 1955

New east facade (above); new entry (facing page)

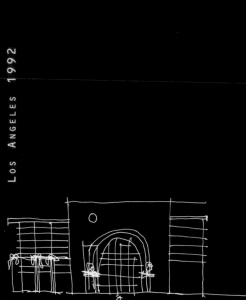

Gilmore Bank Office Building

The new Gilmore Bank and Office Building was
designed for the corner of Third Street and
Fairfax Avenue, opposite the Farmers Market,
when the current site of this one-branch bank
was slated for development. The development
did not proceed, however, and the design for
the "new" bank, at that point in construction
documentation, was shelved. In the final
design the exterior wraps around a two-story
bank chamber with a floor of office space
above. The third-floor office space is set back
from the building edge and perforated by a
skylight that brings light to the bank chamber.
The design of this bank is inspired by Louis
Sullivan's banks and has appropriated strategies
from many of our other projects.

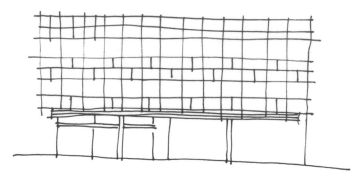

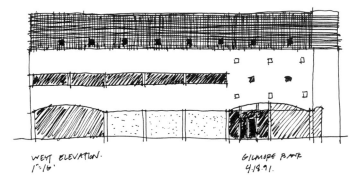

WEST ELEVATION.
1":16'

GILMORE BANK
4.18.91.

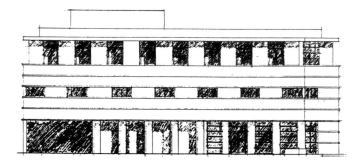

GILMORE
BANK
COMMERCIAL
AND SAVINGS.

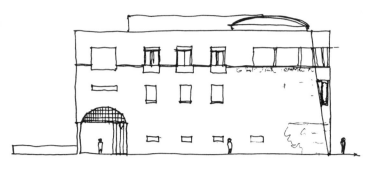

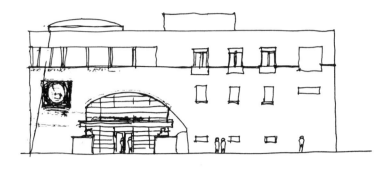

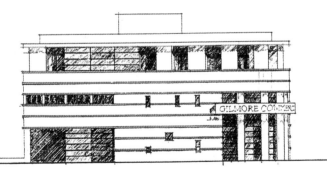

SOUTH ELEVATION · THIRD ST.
1":16'

GILMORE BANK.
4.18.91

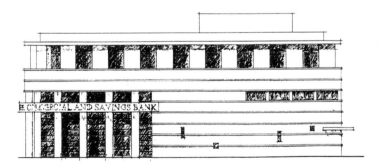

EAST ELEVATION · FAIRFAX.
1":16'

GILMORE BANK.
4.18.91

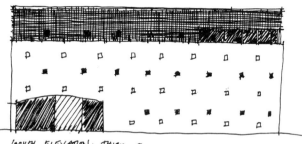

GILMORE COMMERC

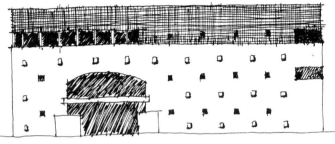

COMMERCIAL AND SAVINGS BANK

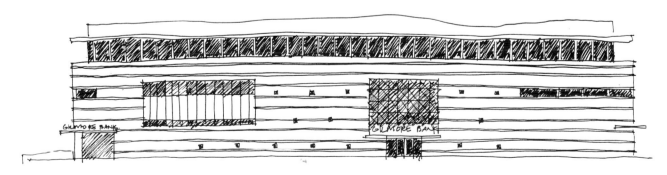

GILMORE BANK

GILMORE BANK

View from Third Street

OP12 / Berkeley Street Housing

"OP" signifies the Ocean Park neighborhood, and "12" refers to twelve units of affordable housing located on two sites, six units on Fifth Street (OP12 5th Street) and six units on Sixth Street (OP12 6th Street). The housing was built for Community Corporation of Santa Monica, a nonprofit housing developer. Berkeley, or Berkeley Street, housing was part of a separate affordable housing program for St. John's Hospital and Health Center, which wished to replace housing units displaced by hospital use. On completion, these units were deeded to the Community Corporation of Santa Monica.

These three housing developments became inextricably linked when they received an award from *Progressive Architecture* in 1987 and the sketches of the three developments were featured on the cover of the magazine, like triplets. It is easy now to see the California modern tradition from which they sprang, exemplified by the work of such architects as Gregory Ain and Irving Gill. At the time, we were too busy watching contemporary architects and learning to run a business to realize we had absorbed this extraordinary California tradition, and we began consciously to get to know it better. Each development followed similar principles. All units are cross-ventilated; open space is organized as a focus rather than a leftover; and standard building components like windows are arranged or grouped in unconventional ways.

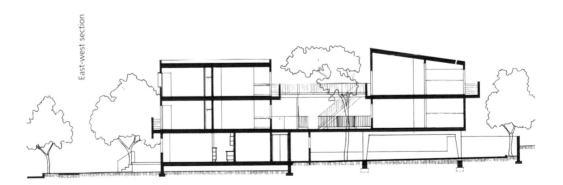

East-west section

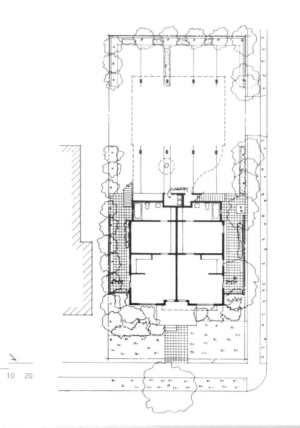

Ground floor plan

0 5 10 20

Second floor plan

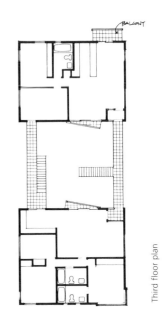

Third floor plan

OP 12 5th Street

Third floor plan

Second floor plan

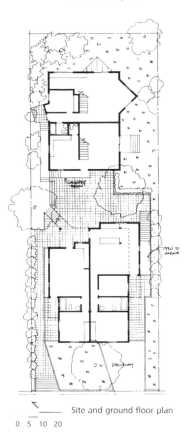

Site and ground floor plan

0 5 10 20

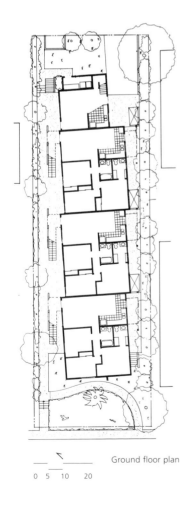

Second floor plan

Berkeley Street

Ground floor plan

0 5 10   20

Electric ArtBlock

In 1988, examples of new work-from-home/artist's housing in the Los Angeles area were few and far between and generally restricted to two- or three-unit projects, like our Hollywood Duplex (p.130). Larger-scale artist's housing developments were generally remodels – converted warehouse/loft spaces. Glenn Erikson, the developer and our architectural colleague on this project, was interested in building artist's loft housing from scratch. The twenty-unit Electric ArtBlock development in the Venice neighborhood was probably the first large-scale, new, artist's loft housing built in Los Angeles. Although the construction of work-from-home housing in areas zoned for commercial and multifamily uses was an objective of the city, banks and codes did not, and still do not, accommodate this building type easily.

The Electric ArtBlock site came bundled with imagery. It was located in mythic Venice, the street name was Electric Avenue, and the site was an abandoned railway easement. The possibilities for architectural cliché were enormous. Envisaging a single, 250-foot-long building (embodying gentrification) across the street from low-income, small apartment buildings was also discomforting. We spent a lot of time organizing the program and the massing into smaller, rhythmical units to make use of the building's length and play off the apartment module, but the building was never intended to be invisible. It will always represent gentrification to many residents, but it has also been accepted affectionately as a local landmark. Its scale is not what you would expect, and its awkwardness takes one by surprise, accurately reflecting the oddity of its legacy and place.

TEXEL
PRINTOLOGY

1291

South elevation

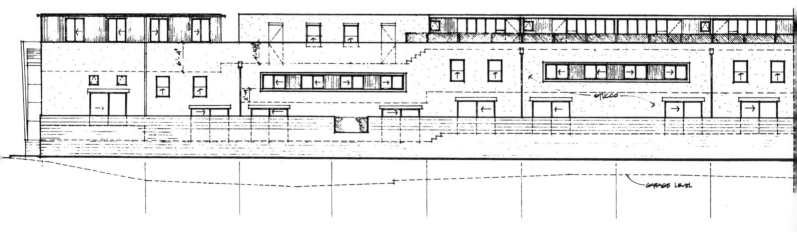

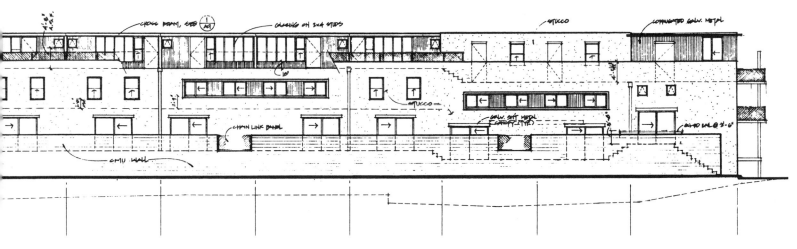

Second floor plan

Mezzanine plan

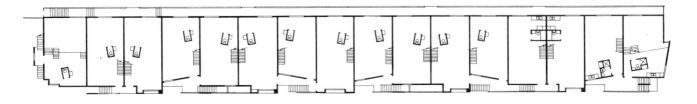

Ground floor plan

0   10   20   40

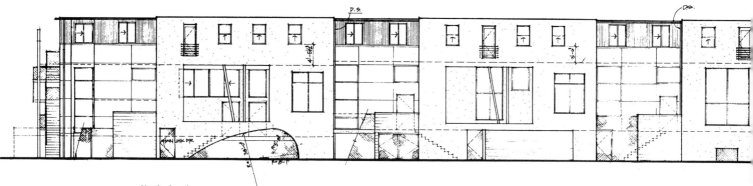

North elevation

McMillen Studio

We were building our own designs when we met artist Mike McMillen. Our combination of skills in both design and construction appealed to him, given his hands-on sensibility gained from making art installations and assemblages and his earlier experience working on special effects for movies. Many of Mike's pieces are anthropomorphic, and it is no surprise that his studio took on an animated quality, although no one of us explicitly sought it. The window trill that runs the length of the building appears in various forms in our work. It was first used here. These windows frame the quintessential horizontal vistas of LA: fragments of buildings, the heads of palm trees, roofs, and sky.

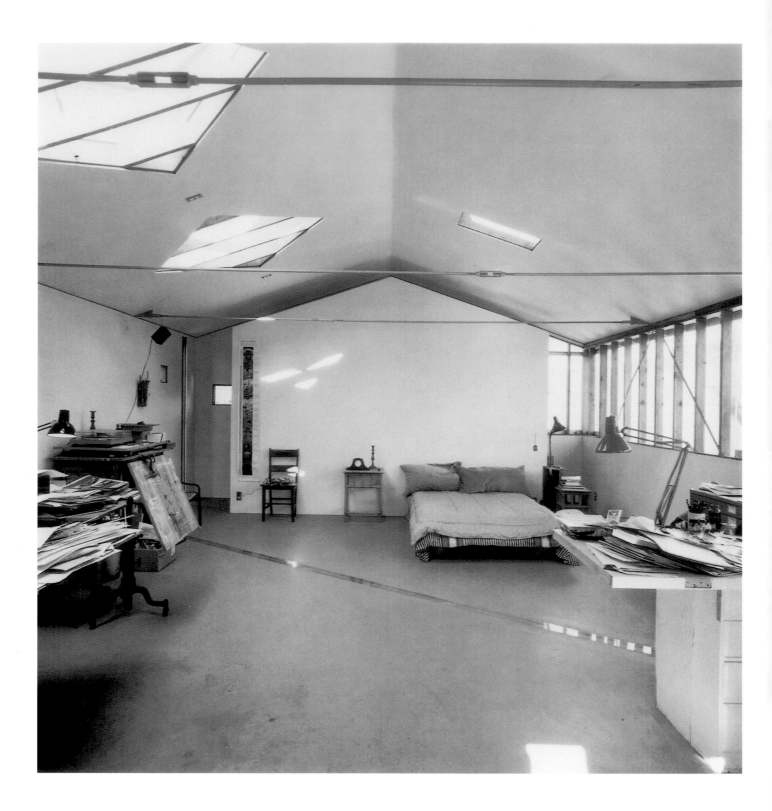

MAR VISTA 1984

SANTA MONICA 1986

Wendel Franzen House

These sliver additions posture more than their programs warrant. In the Rosen House we added a triangular home office entered through a closet; and we added a 10-foot slice of bedroom and family room to the backyard face of the Wendel Franzen cottage. The small scale and theatrical manner of these projects act on their generic vernacular contexts, interpreting and responding to them.

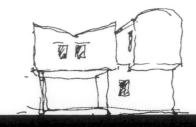

17th Street Addition

We have added space to housing in myriad ways. Two extreme cases are the 17th Street Addition, which adds one and one-half apartments to the alley elevation of a 1960s dingbat apartment building, and the Given Dennis Addition, where a rental unit was added to a California bungalow-style craftsman house.

The 17th Street Addition is an example of the unglamorous but very effective program pursued by the local nonprofit affordable housing developer to rehabilitate deteriorating rental housing. Many of the buildings purchased required only action on deferred maintenance, but in some, such as this one, modifications and additional space were necessary to correct rent control and planning violations. Here the addition formed what the neighborhood children call the cat and mouse.

Given Dennis House Addition

The Given Dennis House was transformed into
a duplex by overlapping one 150-square-foot
existing volume with a 600-square-foot new
one. The wood-clad new volume swallows the
inauspicious older room attached to the side of
the H-plan house.

Lightstorm Entertainment

In low-rise contemporary office building interiors, the limitations of the shell must be addressed and remodels require much artifice. Unlike the voluminous interior of an industrial building, the low height-to-width ratio of generic office space creates a conscious sense of confinement. In remodeling a typical office floor (in this case approximately 10,000 square feet) to accommodate executive workspace for Lightstorm Entertainment, a movie production company, we reshaped the space by raising ceiling heights where possible. We also developed a sequence of layered views that uses light and color to lead the eye to other spaces and the outdoors beyond.

Digital Domain

Utilitarian/industrial buildings, like those
occupied by Digital Domain, a movie industry
special effects company, are voluminous,
unpretentious shells that can accommodate
seemingly ever-changing uses and tenants.
Our work for Digital Domain included creating
movie stages, retrofitting existing generic computer workstations, and designing a screening
room. The screening room design acknowl-
edges the temporary quality and volume of the
building by keeping the shell visible and use-
specific improvements distinct. A few interventions seem permanent, like the purple sound-
isolating/absorbing wall that surrounds the
projection room; but most, like the screen
itself, the seating, and the floor covering, were
treated as temporary artifacts that could be
picked up and moved at short notice.

Molloy House

The California modernist A. Quincy Jones, one of the Case Study architects, designed many houses in Kenter Canyon, including this one. We were asked to add to it to accommodate more bedrooms and bathrooms. The clients are graphic designers and collected vintage modern furniture. Like them, we loved the airiness and ease of the original house. We first attempted to design the addition in the style of the house. The site, however, did not accommodate the type of linear extension appropriate for the style, and the design we generated looked bulky. At the eleventh hour, we suggested a substitute approach that detached the old from the new. The addition pivots around a new curtain-wall bathroom tower and houses the two new bedrooms in a wedge-shaped form dug into the hill. To comply with local design guidelines, the exterior colors are subdued tones; but there was no control on interior colors, which are, as expected, strong.

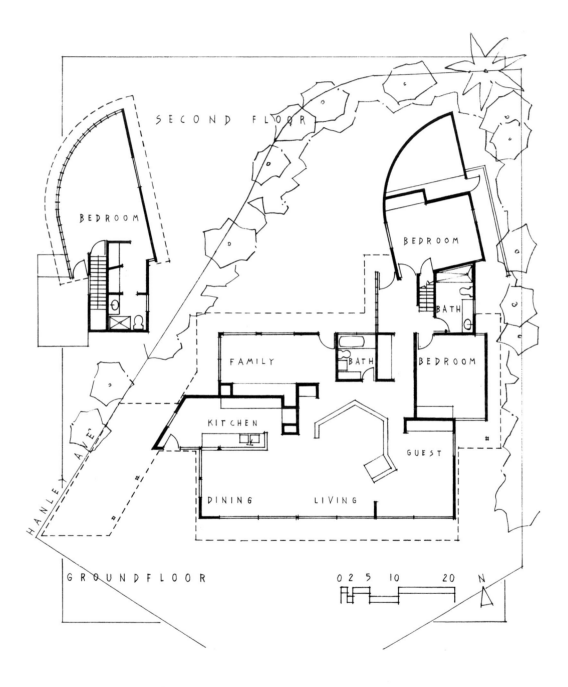

SECOND FLOOR

BEDROOM

BEDROOM

BATH

BATH

FAMILY

BEDROOM

KITCHEN

GUEST

DINING   LIVING

HANLEY AVE.

GROUND FLOOR

0 2 5   10   20   N

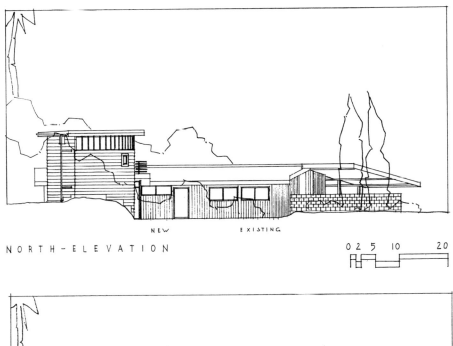

NEW   EXISTING

NORTH-ELEVATION   0 2 5 10 20

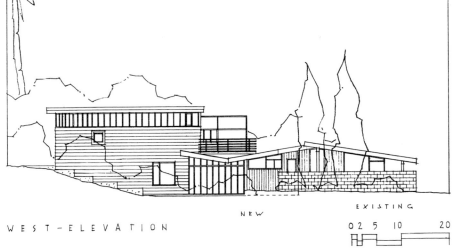

NEW   EXISTING

WEST-ELEVATION   0 2 5 10 20

Ken Edwards Center
for Community Services

It is easy to talk about the "people" aspects
of the city-sponsored Ken Edwards Center for
Community Services: the building houses
community meeting rooms, senior lunch program space, and two nonprofit senior service
providers on the upper floors. We worked
closely with the city and the service providers
to facilitate a sense of community in the building and avoid an institutional atmosphere. As
usual, we configured the building around
shared indoor and outdoor spaces, using
natural light and principles of cross-ventilation
to organize the form.

What now looks to have been easy, but was not, is the accommodation of automobile access requirements and the parking program. Parking is provided not only for building users but also for adjacent businesses, and it required more square footage than the building (25,000 square feet). Most projects in LA start with parking considerations, and usually the entries for cars and pedestrians are isolated from each other. Good street energy can be generated from a balanced interaction between motorists and pedestrians – often places feel very artifical without cars. At the Center it is nice to sit on the side of the pedestrian drop-off area and watch cars and people go by, or to follow the car path to the garage below, past views of streets beyond and daylight on either side of the building.

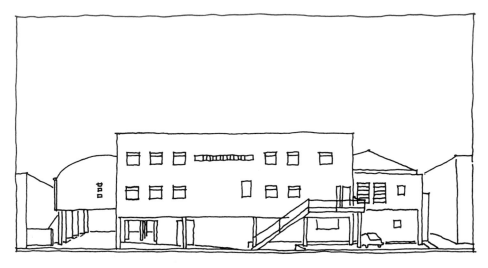

Alley (rear) view

Pedestrian drop-off area

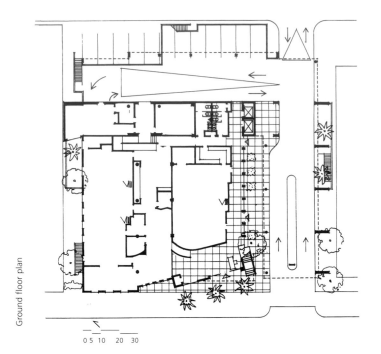

0 5 10   20   30

Second floor plan

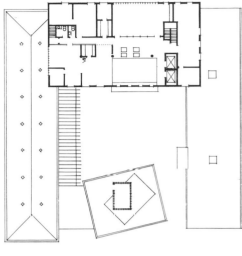

Third floor plan

California Avenue Duplex

The California Avenue Duplex is loaded with idealistic experiments with materials and plan, as befits a first pass at building in California by young architects fresh out of school, who had studied with Charles Moore and were watching Frank Gehry from the corner of their eye. We developed the project ourselves and built it with a friend during a very wet winter. The two units open to a shared courtyard. Our unit in the back, above the parking garage, spread over three levels with very few doors and dramatic spaces, and the front unit is more sensible and serene. We rented the front unit (before it was finished) to an architect friend and his wife, a children's physiotherapist who wanted to work from home. She used the space that opens off the courtyard to work with her clients. It proved to be a very kid-friendly place.

Within a couple of years, both households had children, and the courtyard became the place where they socialized. The duplex was a milestone for us. The organization of our affordable housing projects is greatly influenced by this duplex and our experience there. It revealed the potential of well-structured, shared outdoor space in the design of multiunit housing.

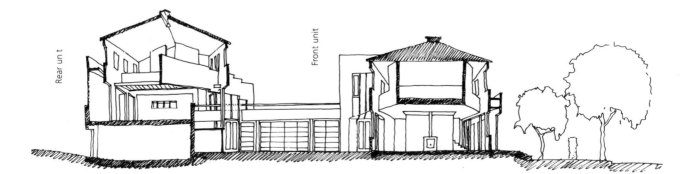

Rear unit

Front unit

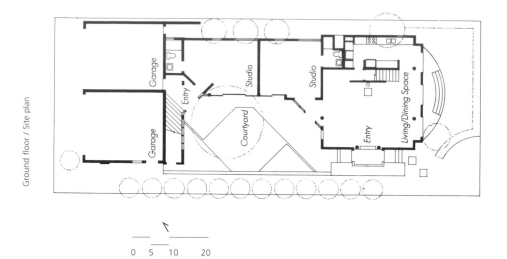

Ground floor / Site plan

Garage

Garage

Entry

Studio

Courtyard

Studio

Entry

Living/Dining Space

0 5 10 20

Mezzanine plan

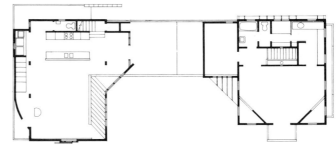

Second floor plan

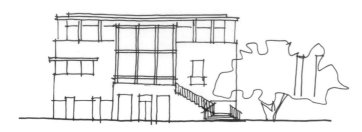

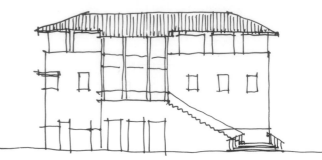

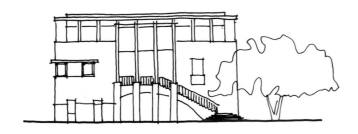

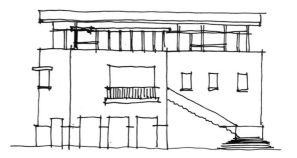

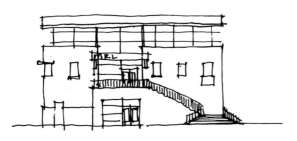

Preliminary sketches

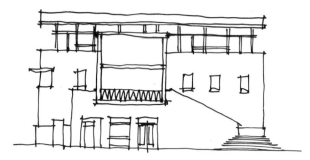

Materials Research Laboratory

The Materials Research Laboratory at UC Santa Barbara is a small building (by campus standards) of 25,000 square feet to be located at the geographical hub of the science quadrant at the edge of the Pacific Ocean. An energetic faculty wants a setting for an innovative inter-disciplinary research program with state-of-the-art laboratories and a creative, collegiate atmosphere. The university wants design issues addressed, including clarified circulation for people, cars, and bicycles, and the consolidation of neighboring buildings of disparate styles (ranging from low-rise neotraditional to mid-rise 1950s modern) into some kind of coherent place.

Our partner architect, Reid Tarics & Associates, was experienced in the building type, while we brought experience in community building and a sensibility toward open space. A simple, solid base of laboratories defines a street to the north and locates its ceremonial front entry on the pedestrian walk. Courtyards to the south and east make positive outdoor places out of leftover space. The upper floors are lacy and contain offices and meeting rooms. The derivation of the design is ambiguous; it slides into and knits together the neighboring buildings. The project is expected to be completed in 1996.

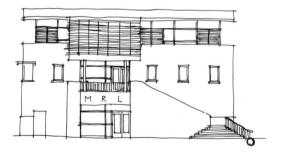

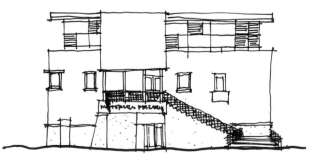

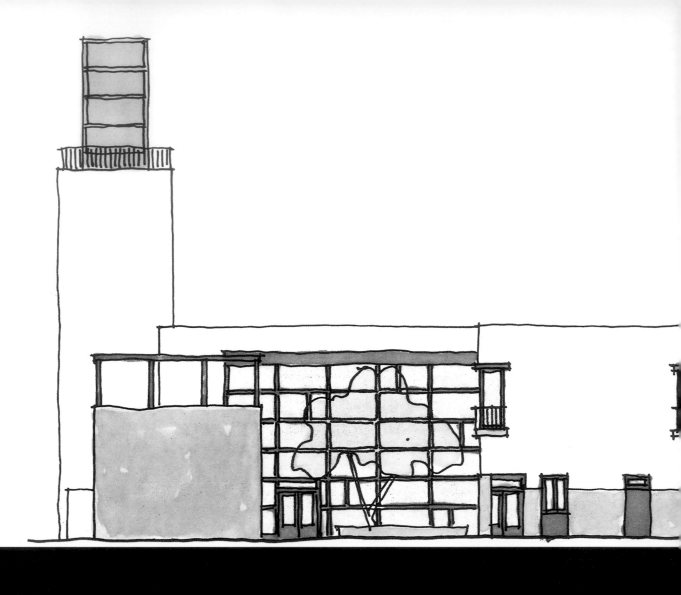

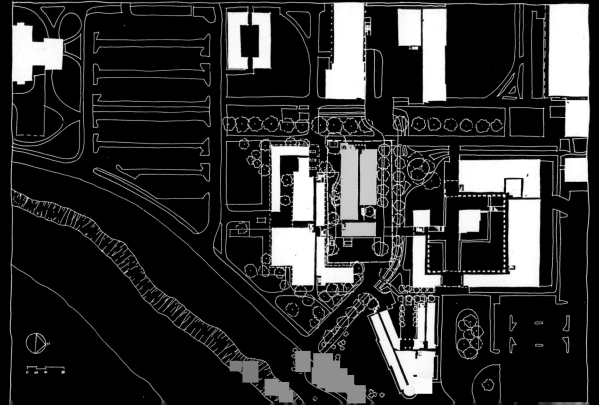

West elevation

Hollywood Duplex

The Hollywood Duplex was a case study in how to make work-from-home housing in the suburbs. We were particularly interested in designing housing in which the aesthetic and life-style of work, rather than of domesticity, dominated. We were both architect and developer for the project.

We had always been fascinated by the way Minoru Yamasaki's two towers in Century City danced around each other, and looking back, we are sure that the dance was part of the study here. Games of closure, surprise, and symmetry also play out in the design; for example, in the modulation, detail, and openness of the hillside view from the rear compared to the tight-lipped, pared-down street view and the exact location of street view openings in both towers. The stair separates the utility spaces – kitchens and bathrooms – from the work/live spaces stacked in a 20' x 20' tower. The stair was conceived and detailed as an outside space, although technically it is enclosed. To get to the top of the building, one loops from outside stair through inside space; each space becomes progressively more domestic and conventional as one moves up through the building.

The landscape has evolved since the project was completed, with the play of simple forms against textured landscape finally in place. The naturalized hillside landscape behind the towers remains and the tipu canopy tree (*Tipuana tipu*) that separates and shades the towers has finally grown in. The mature tree pulls the landscape down toward the street where the naturalized landscape merges with Hollywood's characteristic ornamental Mediterranean planting.

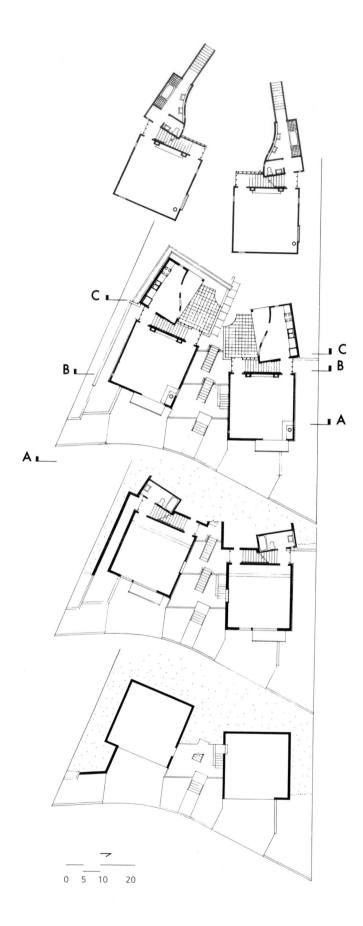

Sleeping

Third floor plan

Living

Second floor plan

Working

First floor plan

Parking

Basement plan

0   5   10   20

Section CC

Section BB

Section AA

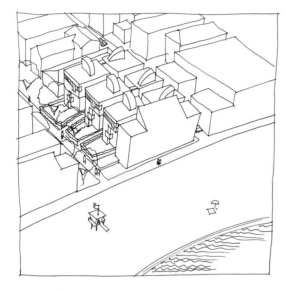

Ozone Beach Boxes

Much of our pragmatism can be attributed to our experiences in the role of developer or builder. We were architect and development partner for the Ozone Beach Boxes, a six-unit condominium project proposed for three contiguous 30' x 110' lots along a Venice neighborhood walk-street (pedestrian access only) just across the alley from the beach. The history of this project is a great case study of development issues in Los Angeles in the late 1980s, which were characterized by a strong no-growth attitude and an equally strong lure to capitalize on booming real estate opportunities. We sold the property after working drawings were complete and it was clear that we would not make our fortune at the tail end of the 1980s real estate boom.

Each condominium was configured as a separate 2,000-square-foot, three-story house plus roof deck with unruly gardens between each unit. Houses facing the walk-street had living spaces on the ground floor opening directly to low-hedged gardens and the street. In the houses facing the alley this layout was inverted, with living spaces on the third floor to gain more dramatic ocean views.

Walk Street Elevation

Walk street

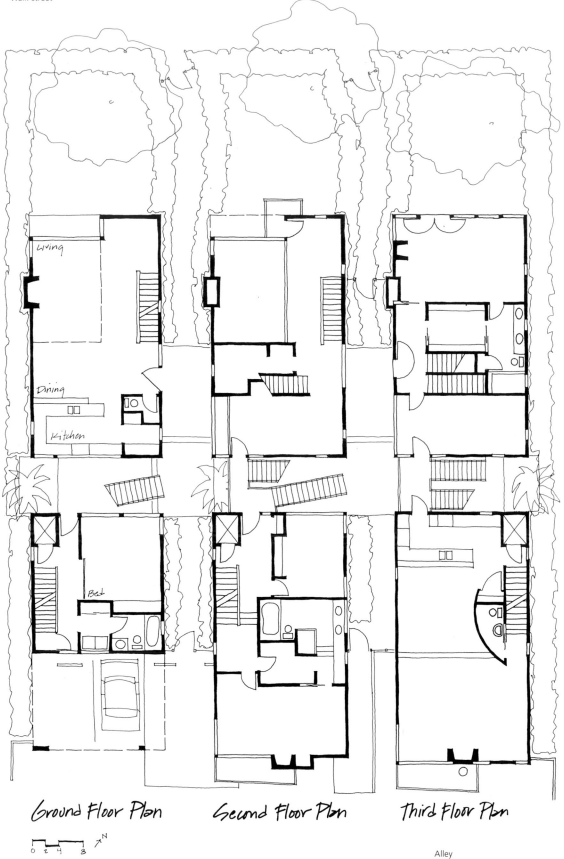

Living

Dining

Kitchen

Bed

Ground Floor Plan   Second Floor Plan   Third Floor Plan

0 2 4 8   N

Alley

144

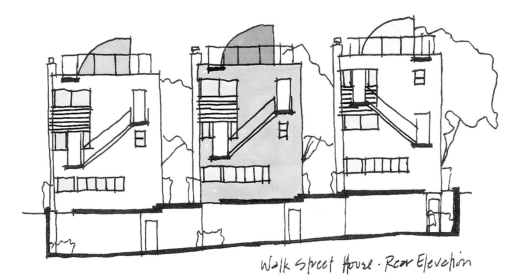

Walk Street House - Rear Elevation

Alley House - Courtyard Elevation

Alley Elevation

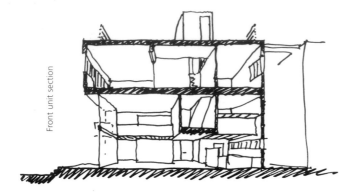

Front unit section

East Elevation

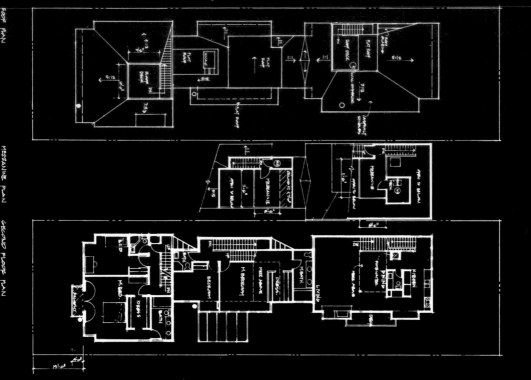

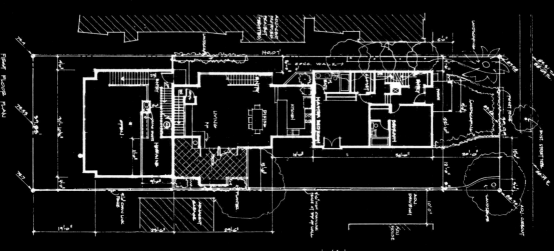

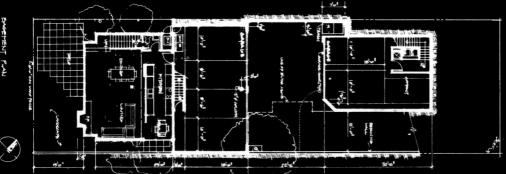

Given Triplex

The Given Triplex is a three-unit speculative condominium development in the Ocean Park neighborhood in Santa Monica. Ocean Park has incentive-based design guidelines that favor pitched roofs in deference to the area's disappearing craftsman-style houses, and the design of the triplex plays with the expectations associated with this tradition. At first glance the triplex appears to be a familiar, craftsman-inspired development with "broad curb appeal," as realtors describe it. Craftsmanlike materials and proportions are used intentionally to solidify the eroding neighborhood texture of the few adjacent older buildings and open spaces; this quiet strategy belies the program's density. On closer inspection, the roof, although pitched, appears not quite conventional, as do the windows. Inside spaces are also unexpectedly voluminous. The idiosyncratic layer is there to add vitality and to confirm – for those who insist that past architecture is better than what we build now – that current architecture may well offer as great a potential as adhering to past traditions.

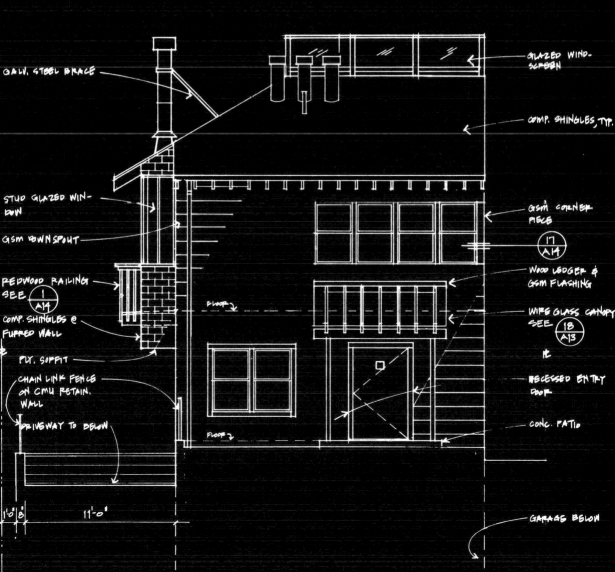

GALV. STEEL BRACE

STUD GLAZED WIN-
DOW

GSM DOWNSPOUT

REDWOOD RAILING
SEE ①
A14

COMP. SHINGLES @
FURRED WALL

PLY. SOFFIT

CHAIN LINK FENCE
ON CMU RETAIN.
WALL

DRIVEWAY TO BELOW

FLOOR 3

FLOOR 2

1'-0" 8"   11'-0"

GLAZED WIND-
SCREEN

COMP. SHINGLES, TYP.

GSM CORNER
PIECE

17
A14

WOOD LEDGER &
GSM FLASHING

WIRE GLASS CANOPY
SEE 18
A13

RECESSED ENTRY
DOOR

CONC. PATIO

GARAGE BELOW

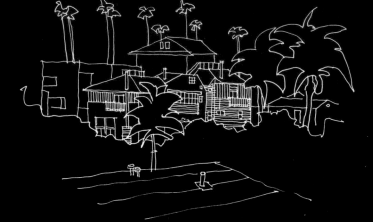

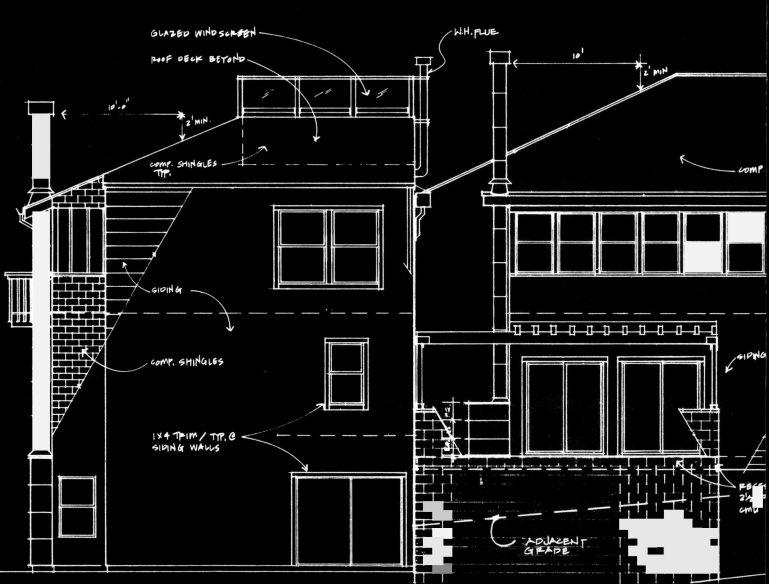

GLAZED WIND SCREEN

ROOF DECK BEYOND

W.H. FLUE

10'

2' MIN

10'-0"

2' MIN.

COMP. SHINGLES
TYP.

COMP

SIDING

COMP. SHINGLES

SIDING

1X4 TRIM / TYP. @
SIDING WALLS

RECE
2½
CMU

ADJACENT
GRADE

MAINTAIN CONSISTENT
16" O.C. MODULE @
ROOF RAFTERS; ALIGN
STUD GLAZED WINDOW
STUDS WITH RAFTERS,
TYP. @ STUD GLAZING.

GSM GUTTER &
D.S.

20
A14

DOWNDRAFT VENT

RECESS'D
ENTRY
BEYOND

PLYWOOD
SOFFIT

WOOD
FASCIA

D.S.

D.S.

RECESS SLAB EDGE
BY 1½" FOR FLUSH
SIDING @ CMU WALL.
SEE
16
A14

EDGE BY
TINUOUS
G

DOWNDRAFT VENT

45° SLAB EDGE
STARTS 12" IN FROM
EDGE OF BUILDING.

NOTE: RETAINING WALL & C.L. FENCE @ P.L. NOT SHOWN FOR CLARITY.

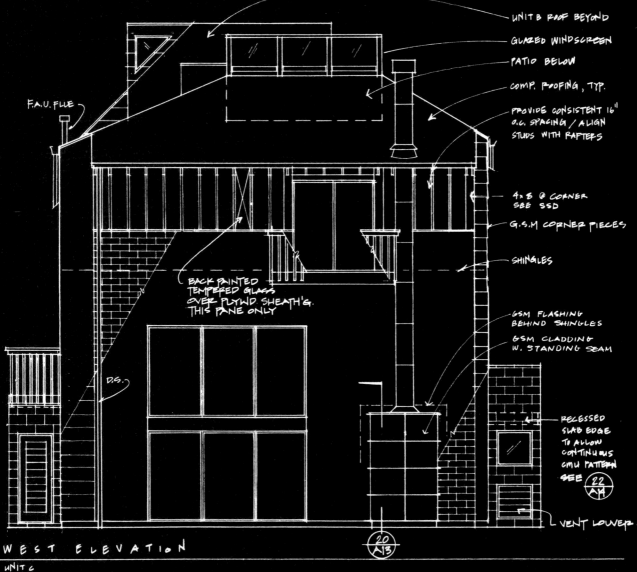

UNIT B ROOF BEYOND

GLAZED WINDSCREEN

PATIO BELOW

COMP. ROOFING, TYP.

PROVIDE CONSISTENT 16"
O.C. SPACING / ALIGN
STUDS WITH RAFTERS

F.A.U. FLUE

4 x 8 @ CORNER
SEE SSD

G.S.M CORNER PIECES

SHINGLES

BACK PAINTED
TEMPERED GLASS
OVER PLYWD SHEATH'G.
THIS PANE ONLY

GSM FLASHING
BEHIND SHINGLES

GSM CLADDING
W. STANDING SEAM

D.S.

RECESSED
SLAB EDGE
TO ALLOW
CONTINUOUS
CMU PATTERN
SEE

22
A14

VENT LOUVER

3
A11

WEST ELEVATION
UNIT C

20
A13

154

Koning Eizenberg House

The 2,700-square-foot Koning Eizenberg
House is skinny, only seventeen feet wide
along most of its length, with many moving
parts: oversized exterior sliding glass doors,
hinged french doors, secret and surface interior
sliding doors, Australian sashless windows, and
rolling wood shutters. It strongly reflects
Hank's ingenuity and interest in making and
operating things and our desire for the house
to open up to the outside to accommodate
an easy life-style for us, our two children,
and our dog.

The outside is the big space, and the
house the backdrop. As such, the house was
designed to be obscured by landscape, offering
only glimpses of itself rather than an overall
image (see photo p. 206). As in many of our
houses, the organization of the garden and its
open space generated the form of the house.
Planting is also used to maximize comfort. For
example, the arbor, now grown over, shades
the southeast-facing glass wall that opens
to the garden.

0   5   10   20

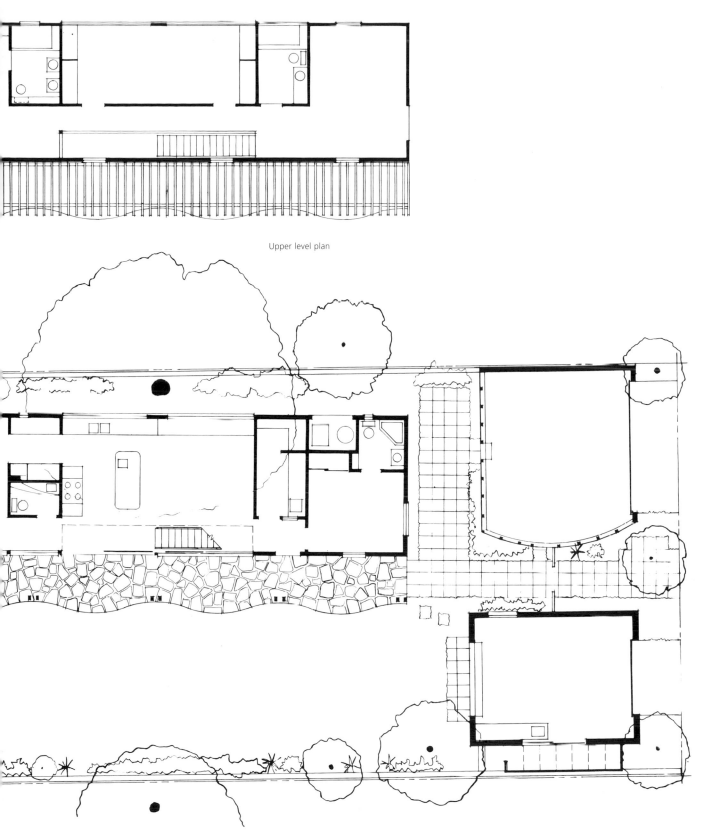

Upper level plan

Site plan

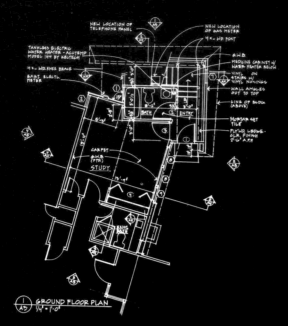

① GROUND FLOOR PLAN
A3 ¼" = 1'-0"

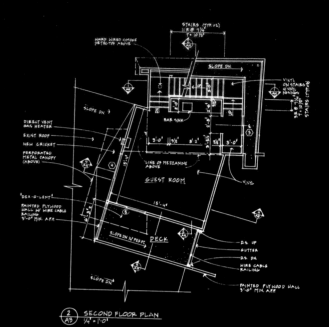

② SECOND FLOOR PLAN
A3 ¼" = 1'-0"

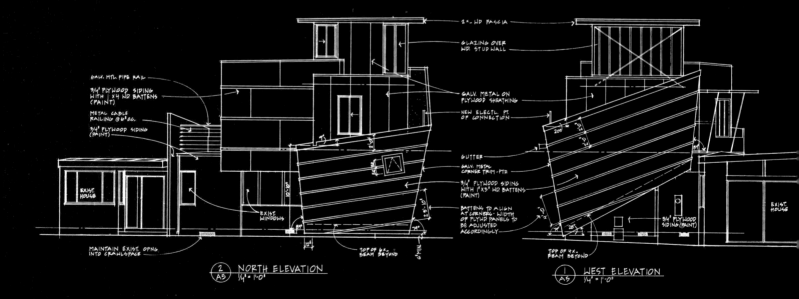

② NORTH ELEVATION
A3 ¼" = 1'-0"

① WEST ELEVATION
A3 ¼" = 1'-0"

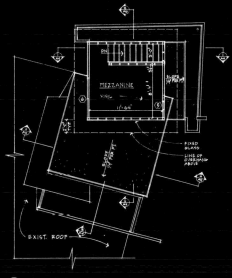

$\dfrac{3}{A3}$ MEZZANINE PLAN $\frac{1}{4}" = 1'-0"$

Moore's Folly

Moore's Folly is a carefree project that added a small (700 square feet) three-story guest room to a ranch-style house in Malibu. The family that lived in the house collected art and animals, and it was not uncommon for their horse to wander inside the house. The apartment, through osmosis rather than conventional design, evolved into a kind of ark, perfectly scaled for giraffes.

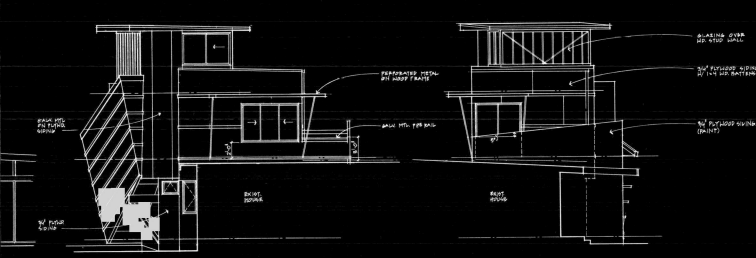

Erenberg House

Elena and Sam Erenberg are artists who wished to work from home. They bought a modest, traditional Spanish-style house down the road from ours. They chose to leave the house pretty much intact and direct attention to obtaining studio space and optimizing the garden space. As with the design of the 31st Street House (p. 180), we walked a fine line between the prosaic and the heroic, playing with expectations of scale and the plasticity of stucco. The clients were interested in the potential of color, and we worked together to achieve the vibrant contrast between the courtyard colors and the new stuccoed volume. The red paint is the same red we used inside our house, and it was great to see the color escape down the street. The roof deck is the best place to appreciate the power of the color, as one climbs up the red stair within red balustrade walls and suddenly confronts a blue sky.

NORTH ELEVATION

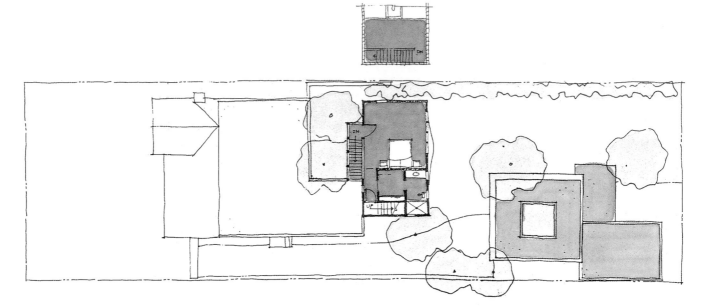

Second floor plan

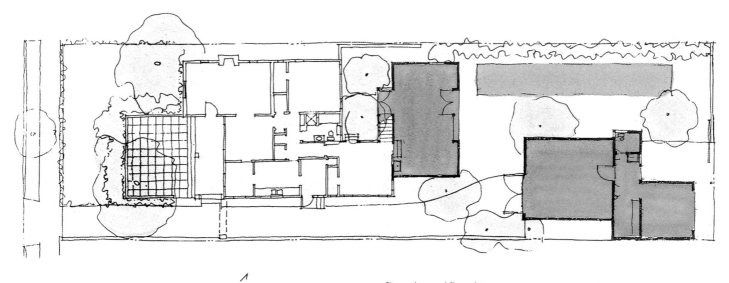

Site and ground floor plan

0   8   16

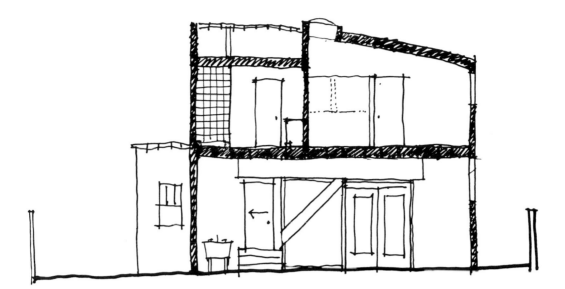

SECTION — ELENA'S STUDIO

1/8" = 1'-0"   8.27.93   KEA
9.10.93

EAST ELEVATION — ELENA'S STUDIO
9.10.93   KEA

31st Street House

The Valli-Marills are friends of ours. Our children went to preschool together; we had spent time at their house and had a good sense of how they lived; they had seen our house and liked it. Nevertheless, when they wanted to expand their 1,300-square-foot house, we were not sure that they thought we would be interested or suitable architects for the project. Perhaps they were afraid that their budget was too small and that an architect-designed addition might make their house uncomfortably conspicuous in this modest neighborhood. It became apparent that the Valli-Marills's desire to be inconspicuous had nothing to do with fear of an unconventional design sensibility but was rather a response to budget and

planning controls, both of which limited the number of square feet that could be added to the house. In the end, everything that existed was remodeled and 650 square feet were added – essentially the two-story portion of the house. Covered outdoor space was not limited by code, and the covered dining area was created to augment the limited entertaining area.

It is clear that in this house we played out our interest in extracting the extraordinary out of the ordinary suburban context and making the commonplace art. With this kind of architecture the architect must understand the compositional and ornamental language of a given context in order to achieve a primary interpretation that slides invisibly into a location. The secondary interpretation is framed to be discovered. In our case, it relies on manipulating conventional expectations of the sequence of indoor and outdoor spaces, color, scale, and ornament.

Before

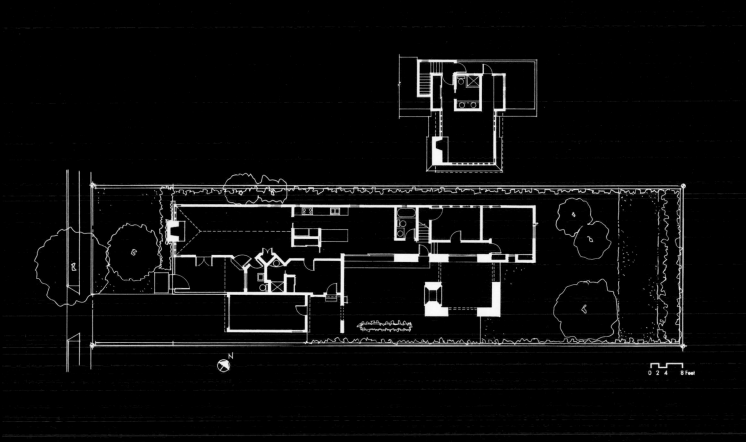

0 2 4 8 Feet

Original plan

Tarzana House

The 3,000-square-foot, three-bedroom Tarzana
House is located in the San Fernando Valley,
north of the Santa Monica Mountains. Tarzana
is a rustic subdivision with sprawling residential
lots and big trees. It takes its name from
Tarzan, in honor of an early resident who
dreamed up the famous fictional character.
Before Tarzana became a shady irrigated suburb, it was probably a landscape of fruit
groves, and before that, desert – like most
of LA. The house, designed for a doctor,
became a medium for exploring the changes
in landscape that characterize the region's
development. The dry motor and entry courts
transmute through the house into a shady,
green, irrigated garden.

The house is essentially transitional
shelter rather than enclosure. In fact, the most
roomlike place on the site is outdoors – the
yellow-walled entry courtyard. Interest in the
inversion of inside and outside had been brew-
ing in our work for some time. Many projects
had outside spaces appropriated as inside
spaces – the entry hall in our own house, for
example (p. 154), and the stairs in the
Hollywood Duplex (p. 130). We explored the
reverse for the first time in the Tarzana House,
appropriating a traditional inside space, the
walled room, as an outside space.

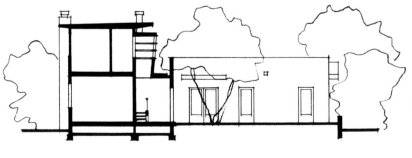

Section

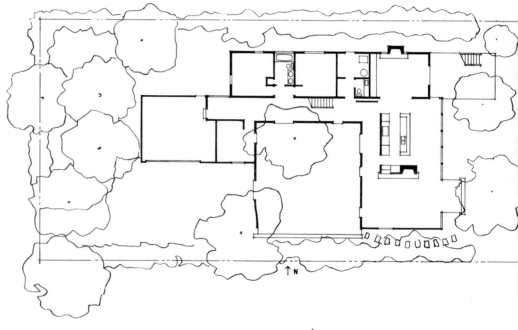

Second floor plan

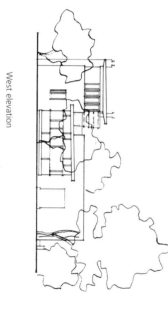

West elevation

Ground floor plan

0 4 8 16

South elevation

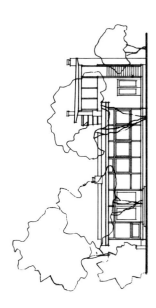

East elevation

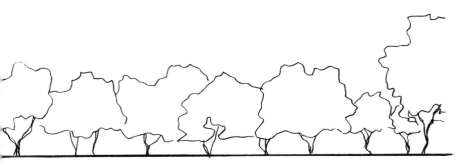

...a leaf of grass is no less than the journey-work of the stars.

–Walt Whitman, *Song of Myself*

Koning Eizenberg House, Santa Monica (photo 1996)

Cheap Thrills and Double Takes

Julie Eizenberg

Like many architects, we have spent a lot of time making a little money build big ideas. We have an affinity for cheap materials and building components and have pursued ways of reassembling them that appear effortless and nontraditional. (Or are they?) Sunlight, air, and natural beauty provide us with compositional direction and ornament. A tree, for example, can be cheap shade and ornamentation if you have a little patience. Sunlight is there for the taking; and the wind, although invisible, changes the ambience of a place as surely as does a turn in conversation: "There was a desert wind blowing that night. It was one of those hot dry Santa Ana's that come down through the mountain passes and curl your hair and make your nerves jump and your skin itch."[1]

In looking back, it seems that a confluence of interests and opportunity has generated our particular way of interpreting a given context. I know that architects are trained to think of context as an objective, rational framework and use it to justify design decisions and fix meaning to design.

1 Raymond Chandler, *Red Wind* (1934; reprint, New York: Ballantine Books, 1980), p. 187.

206

I don't believe this for a minute. Contexts are interpreted, not objective, phenomena. The painter Edward Hopper, for example, suggests a morose and hopeless aura in his views of the countryside. No one would expect him to have painted a cheerful view just because he was painting a street in town. Why, then, are architects expected to reinvent themselves from place to place? We need to acknowledge that architects bring a particular point of view with them from site to site. It is time to put aside the conventionalized and trivial idea of contextualism – of buildings "fitting" into, rather than acting on, a place.

Our view of any context is colored by an economy of means, opportunities to manipulate the experiential qualities of light, air, and nature, interest in creating the perception of effortlessness and the unexpected, and an intense desire to build (which adds a pragmatic, straightforward bent). Add to this myriad other influences: film clips, fragmentary views from trains and momentary glimpses through gates into courtyards beyond (in Italy, France, Mexico), other architects' work, arguments, art, colleagues, our children, our parents, paper ornaments (from China, Mexico, Newberry's), and past projects.

I distrust thematic interpretations of a place that focus on an idealized and romanticized view of existing buildings, ornamentation, and scale. Such interpretations fix a place for all time, frozen, in fancy dress. I prefer to focus on more ambivalent aspects of place – like the spaces between things or everyday phenomena – and to find a way to highlight them. Can architecture frame ordinary things so they can be appreciated much the same way in which David Hockney's paintings made the backyard sprinkler seem extraordinary, and Ed Ruscha's art legitimized parking lots and apartment buildings, without romanticizing or deifying them, and permitted us to see gas stations as an evocative medium?

The 1994 competition to design a cultural history museum in Victoria, Australia, provided us with an opportunity to explore conventional expectations of context. We did not win the competition, but in truth,
I am not surprised. Our entry, like much of our recent work, highlighted relationships rather than buildings. The museum site is in a European-style park of mature deciduous trees in an inner suburb of Melbourne characterized by nineteenth-century row houses and low-scale, mixed-use buildings. In the middle of the park is an enormous domed exhibition building dating from 1880, when Melbourne was a bustling metropolis of about 280,000 people at the edge of the colonial world. The new museum program called for keeping the historic exhibition building and proposed an additional 300,000 square feet of exhibition and operation space.

The combination of the setting and the cultural history program was provocative to us. It called into question the relationship of past and present time, old and new, the introduced and the indigenous, and the contributions of different cultures.

Australian history traditionally has depicted the country's indigenous culture, landscape, and fauna as exotic. From the Aboriginal frame of reference, however, this interpretation must seem quite the reverse. This insight suggested a new context for the museum: We now imagined the heroic exhibition building in a precolonial landscape ringed in turn by the cultivated city. Consequently, in the competition entry the exhibition building sits unchanged in native eucalyptus woodland, not a European garden, flanked by new simple forms that house the additional program. Which is more exotic, the past or the present? Which is more extraordinary, the eucalyptus woodland or the exhibition building?

Many contemporary architects, like the modernists who preceded them, exude a confidence of purpose and interpretation that I do not share. I would like to believe in the universal communicative power of architecture, yet my dad is right: traditional houses do sell better. Experience suggests that not everybody sees architecture the way architects do. Everyday experiences like having dinner at a friend's "nondesigned" house, and hearing my children tell me that their house is weird (but cool), reinforce my belief that postmodernism, for all its talk of shared meanings, could not address the fascinating gap between popular culture and its artifacts, and architecture and its artifacts. I am increasingly interested in the physical and psychological relationship between vernacular/nondesigned contexts – defined by the conventional expectations of popular culture – and architects' design interventions. For me this interaction is as interesting as the buildings and artifacts themselves.[2]

For us, the building is a framework that allows many things to happen and in turn relies on them to be complete. What if architecture were not the focus of attention in a building but an incidental discovery? A second glance at a seemingly ordinary building might reveal something – a color or a detail – that changes the viewer's perception, so that an ordinary scene becomes extraordinary, an effect similar to that of the plot unfolding in Alfred Hitchcock's *Rear Window*. A change in the viewer's frame of reference might trigger an unfolding sequence of architectural moves. Architecture does not always have to be outspokenly heroic. It can be subversive, ephemeral, discovered.

It is difficult to unravel how this sketchy point of view has been translated into building design. It is informed by our experience building and by at least three apprenticeships – one in formal composition, another in the structure of the ordinary environment and vernacular building styles, and another in landscape architecture.

We began our apprenticeship in formal composition with Professor George Stiny at UCLA in 1979; it started with the proposition that design is a thought process that can be modeled algorithmically. Algorithms are the structures that underlie computer computation. At that time the arts establishment viewed computers as anathema and shape grammars[3] – part of the design algorithm model and our area of study – as something curious but creatively deadening; in their view, math and art could not and should not mix. Today computers are recognized as creatively liberating, and design algorithms and shape grammars are viewed with interest. Things change.

2 I am inspired by artist John Baldessari's mind-bending juxtapositions of objects, words, and events that seem to undermine conventional ways of seeing things. His *Floating: Color* (1972), for example, comprises six photographic prints, each showing a different colored sheet of paper floating in front of an old house. Neither the paper nor the house is special, yet combined, neither is ordinary. Moreover, the colored paper and the house are linked by a space between them that is revealed in their relationship.
3 George Stiny, "Introduction to shape and shape grammars," *Environment and Planning B*, vol. 7 (1980a): 343-51.

K. E. A. defocused designs

K. E. A. shape grammar

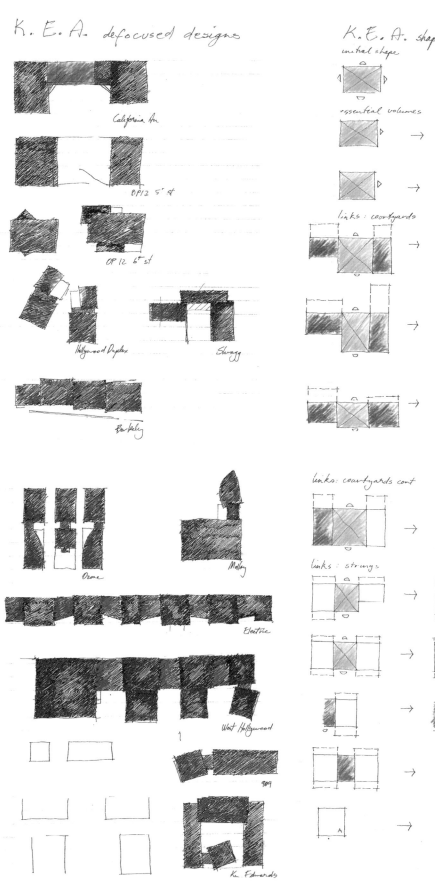

California Av

OP13 5' st

OP 12 6th st

Hollywood Duplex

Shragg

Berkeley

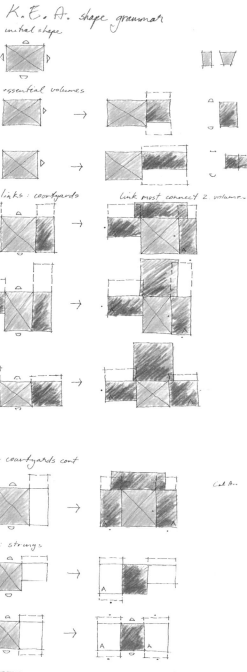

initial shape

essential volumes

links: courtyards   link must connect 2 volumes

links: courtyards cont

Cal Av

links: strings

Orone

Mallory

Electric

West Hollywood

909

Ken Edwards

The beginning of a Koning Eizenberg Architecture shape grammar, 1989 —
our buildings always start with an open space.

A shape grammar is a recursive formalism that defines a language of design (mine, yours, Frank Lloyd Wright's, Le Corbusier's) in terms of visual composition and ornamental structure – its shapes and spatial relations. Think about it: How can one architect's work be distinguished from another's unless it exhibits a consistent, conscious or subconscious, selection of a limited range of visual elements and ways of assembling them? The shapes and spatial relations that generate designs in a language are not necessarily explicit in the designs, although they may be. The language and its grammar are in essence defined by a designer to appear as complex or as ordered, or as whimsical as desired, and an infinite variety of languages is possible and expected.

4 T. W. Knight, "Shape Grammars and Color Grammars in Design," *Environment and Planning B*, vol. 21 (1994): 705-35.
5 H. Koning and J. Eizenberg, "The Language of the Prairie: Frank Lloyd Wright's Prairie Houses," *Environment and Planning B*, vol. 8 (1981): 295-323.
6 See the new "Frank Lloyd Wright" house in William J. Mitchell's essay in this book, p. 11.

Shape grammars have been used in the arts and architecture as an analytical tool and generative mechanism with powerful results.[4] Hank and I investigated their analytical potential in the design of a three-dimensional grammar that generated the compositional forms of Frank Lloyd Wright's prairie houses.[5] The test of an analytical grammar is not just to account for the forms and functions of case study examples (in this case, eleven houses) but also to generate new designs that are considered acceptable designs in the language.[6] This work had a profound effect on us. The concept of grammars legitimizes the formal aspects of design, demanding that they be consciously addressed and not buried in program and contextual response. Form follows intent, not function. Moreover, one is freed to think of architecture as made up of discrete, nonhierarchical languages allowing one the security of investigating or acknowledging other languages without feeling that one has compromised one's own.

Much of our second apprenticeship was spent (not surprisingly) learning another design language – the language of the ordinary environment and the vernacular as seen, for example, at the Farmers Market, a Los Angeles cultural landmark of mythic proportions – the stuff of postcards. Over a period of more than ten years it has been our job to seamlessly repair the market and consolidate its operations without gentrifying it. The market is a formalized collection of market stalls where fruit, produce, souvenirs, dry goods, and prepared food (eaten on the shady patios) are sold. The buildings, in fact, are not beautiful, although the general perception of them is very romanticized. Their style is best described as "state fair rural," and the paving is asphalt. It is the ad hoc compositional structure, people, and merchandise that enliven the whole.

We consolidated our study of the vernacular by quietly building additions to Spanish-style, Dutch colonial-style, and craftsman houses around town. I remember young, idealistic architects and potential employees visiting our office who were extremely disturbed by our fascination with traditional vernacular styles, as if buildings that had roots outside modernism had less value today. I view modernism as a great experiment. At this point, however, it is essentially just one more historical source from which to draw. I do not understand the fuss.

Our fascination with vernaculars is not motivated by ornament or sentiment: it extends also to many contemporary, nondesigned places like tented buildings waiting to be fumigated, and strip centers. I know these centers are ugly, but in LA they are alive with activity and economic opportunity. More disturbing to me are the many well-

planned and tasteful buildings and places that have no vitality, such as the ubiquitous office buildings with slick plazas and lobbies and entrances flanked by two rows of trees and floral borders. In the pursuit of designing and controlling everything in these places, designers have rubbed away all rawness and energy.

Our third apprenticeship, discovering the potential of landscape, dates to undergraduate days in Australia in the early 1970s. Hank and I took a side trip from architecture into forestry, studying forest conservation and the classification and identification of trees. Five years later, when we arrived at UCLA, William Mitchell and Charles Moore were writing *The Poetics of Gardens,* and we jumped at the chance to visit, research, and draw gardens and natural landscapes for their book. Simultaneously we reinforced our knowledge of the experiential qualities of path, sequence, light, shade, shadow, void, contrast, scale, and time. It became clear that whatever one could do formally and ornamentally with bricks and mortar, one could do with nature. Moreover, plant material is not perceived as artificial no matter how deliberate or contrived its organization. This aspect of landscape appealed to our growing interest in the perception and structure of the nondesigned.

By the time we had collaborated with landscape architect Robert Fletcher on our house in Santa Monica in 1989 and the Tarzana House in 1992, we were fairly directed about the potential of landscape in our work. Nevertheless, once you walk a site with Bob, you never see the outdoors in quite the same way again. A great plant man and visionary, Bob introduced us to plant combinations and materials we had never seen, to the modern California landscape tradition of Thomas D. Church and Ralph Cornell, and to a better appreciation of the seasonal – and particularly long-term – life cycle of gardens. One must assume that landscape, unlike buildings, will change. No planting is fixed or complete, although at any one point in time it may appear so.

Starting out as architect-builders, we were involved in both the design and construction of many small residential projects. We quickly learned how unreceptive the building industry and individual trades were to nonstandard installations and applications. No matter how familiar the component or how logical the presumed money-saving strategy, unconventional applications of materials and components carry hidden labor costs unless one does the work oneself. Something that looks inexpensive may not be: glazed, exposed stud work is one example. It appears to be a cheap, effortless, creative use of conventional frame-wall construction, but stud framing is conventionally concealed in the wall and is the domain of the rough carpenter. When exposed, this work is the domain of the finish carpenter and is much more expensive. Moreover, the glazing over the studs is considered custom work and is therefore costlier. Such differences between the perception and reality of construction came as quite a surprise to us.

Rather than inhibiting our efforts, the knowledge gained fed our interest in beating the construction system with its own rules. Affordable housing was our opportunity to test that knowledge and to design larger buildings that would be built. I did not realize in the mid-1980s that it was so unconventional to experiment with the form and aesthetics of this building type or to admit that you liked people. We were interested in making housing that afforded opportunities for people to casually establish friendships and a sense of belonging. We used courtyards and shared outdoor and indoor spaces to frame such opportunities. Affordable housing is much needed in the U.S. and, given the rigor of construction budgets and the multiple bureaucratic constraints on this building type, a challenging problem for architects. Nevertheless, it is even more challenging for the developers, who draw on an ever-diminishing source of funds. Even when land costs are not factored in the overall cost, it is difficult, if not impossible, to make affordable rents offset development and operating costs in large cities like Los Angeles. The affordable housing crisis in the U.S. cannot be solved by the ingenuity of architects, as modernism promised. No inventive building system or clever planning strategy can cover the budgetary shortfall without an increased commitment of government funds and creative financing on a large scale.

At times architecture seems astonishingly esoteric and out of touch with reality, a point we tried to make in the 1993 "The Architect's Dream: Houses for the Next Millenium" exhibition at the Contemporary Arts Center in Cincinnati, Ohio, for which architects were asked to design dream houses. The museum's request seemed extraordinary considering that fewer and fewer people in the United States at that time were able to participate in the dream of home ownership. Ours was an office of seven people, and only Hank and I owned our own home. After much discussion we all came to the conclusion that, given economic reality, a dream house was something most people could not have. For the exhibition each person in the office provided an image of where he or she lived at the time, along with a vision of their "dream house."

Architectural idealism and everyday reality collided again in 1994 in our *House, 20 June 1994* in the "House Rules" exhibition at the Wexner Center in Columbus, Ohio. Ten architect/social theorist teams including Koning Eizenberg Architecture (teamed with bell hooks) were asked to explore, through words and a model, the form and nature of the single-family detached house, given that, as the curator wrote, "diverse compositions of 'family' have called into question long-standing assumptions about the home and its configuration."[7] Demographics indeed suggest that traditional families (mom, dad, and children) make up fewer and fewer households in the U.S. today, while the number of households comprised of single

Opposite page, from Koning Eizenberg Architecture's piece, *What Would Your Dream House Be?*, in "The Architect's Dream" exhibition at the Contemporary Arts Center in Cincinnati, 1993. *Details*, by:

1
Hank Koning, Julie Eizenberg, both 39 years old, married, 2 children. Principals, Koning Eizenberg Architecture, 12 years.

2
Neil Peoples, 28 years old, cohabiting. At Koning Eizenberg Architecture 2$^1/_2$ years.

3
Heidi Williams, 35 years old, married, 1 child. At Koning Eizenberg Architecture 8 years.

4
Mark Schoeplein, 30 years old, cohabiting. At Koning Eizenberg Architecture 4 years (on and off).

7 Mark Robbins, "Building Like America: Making Other Plans," *Assemblage 24* (August 1994): 8.

1

2

3

4

5 *Detail:*
Mike Ching, 30 years
old, single. At Koning
Eizenberg Architecture
9 months.

6 *Detail:*
Tim Andreas, 29 years
old, dating. At Koning
Eizenberg Architecture
6 years.

parents and children, single-gender cohabitants, and single people is increasing. Ethnicities and life-styles vary widely, and increasingly people work from home. The residential building type, however, reflects little of this demographic change and variety. Our response to this situation and architects' ability to address this change is summed up in my letter to bell hooks:

Dear bell,

This Wexner thing has been frustrating for me because I believe that the form of single-family houses is controlled by planning regulations, banks, economics, and structures for the protection of personal assets. It is these controls that truly limit the opportunity to adapt the single-family house to a variety of lifestyles beyond the nuclear family. It's not architects at all.

These controls need to change. When we spoke the other day, I was angry with architects' lack of reality about what effects change in the real world. And to make that point, I didn't want to build a model of any house. But you are right, without a vision of what the change can accomplish, I have said nothing. I read your letters and the essay again and also thought about why you chose to work with us. You liked the buildings, not any social agenda, and buildings are important places for you – they allow for dreams and freedom. So now I have built a house. I hope to facilitate your dreams – and the dreams of others.

Julie

Santa Monica, California

The letter, excerpts from planning regulations, a will, real estate comparables, a bank appraisal form, and a loan application are inscribed on the plexiglass vitrine that encases our utopian, but currently illegal, house proposal.

The "House Rules" exhibition was installed adjacent to work by artists. In looking from artists' to architects' work, it was clear to me that architects liked to explain. I prefer art and architecture that is more open-ended and offers a visceral or subliminal connection to the viewer first, subordinating explicit explanation to the catalog notes. To prescribe an interpretation of a building one must assume a correct response and a set of conventions shared by the maker and the viewers. Observations of multicultural LA confirm my experience: life is more complicated and richer than this assumption. Conveying meaning in architecture is more likely a controlled statistical gamble given the diversity of the viewers' experiences. This point of view confirms the pluralism suggested by shape grammar theory that supports many approaches to architecture – not one right one.

We want reality to work. We want to work reality, to improve the city in order to keep the wilderness and stop the sprawl. We do not see the need to build a new system from scratch. Modern cities are not always pretty, but there is a lot of potential in "everyday urbanism."[8] We would like to believe that architecture can positively affect a community's self image. We want it acknowledged that a good building raises the spirit at least as much as does a good movie. Like many architects before us, we are motivated by the simple pleasures of light, air, and natural beauty as well as architecture's potential to reframe the everyday. We are also increasingly interested in the double take that reveals the unexpected and extraordinary hidden within contemporary commonplace contexts. LA is a great place for such research.

8   This term refers to the collective aspects of everyday life, from going to the laundromat to commuting to work, coupled with the idea that activities, not just buildings, structure space. It is developed in Margaret Crawford, John Kaliski, and John Chase, *Everyday Urbanism – LA Forum for Architecture and Urban Design* (forthcoming; to be published with a grant from the Graham Foundation).

June 20, 1994

Dear bell

This Wexner thing has been frustrating to me because I believe
that the form of single family houses is controlled by planning
regulations, banks, economics, and structures for the
protection of personal assets. It is these controls that truly limit
the opportunity to adapt the single family house to a variety of
lifestyles beyond the nuclear family. It's not architecture at all.

These controls need to change. When we spoke the other day,
I was angry with architects' lack of reality about what effects
change in the real world and to make that point I didn't want
to build a model of any house. But you are right, without a
vision of what the change can accomplish, I have said nothing.
I read your letters and the essay again and also thought about
why you chose to work with us. You liked the buildings, not
any social agenda, and buildings are important places for you –
they allow for dreams and freedom. So now I have built a
house. I hope to facilitate your dreams – and the dreams
of others.

Selected Projects

All projects are in California unless otherwise noted.

Institutional Educational

Materials Research Laboratory (with Reid Tarics & Associates), University of California at Santa Barbara, 1996
Research/office facility, 25,000 sq. ft.

Peck Park Recreation Center Gymnasium, San Pedro, 1996, 12,000 sq. ft.

Sepulveda Recreation Center Gymnasium, Los Angeles,1995, 10,500 sq. ft.

Ken Edwards Center for Community Services, Santa Monica, 1990, 25,000 sq. ft.

PS 1 Elementary School, Santa Monica, 1986, 1991, 1994–96; exterior improvements and remodel, master planning for 20,000 sq. ft. new school

Alternative Living for the Aging (ALA) Senior Service Center, West Hollywood, 1986
Office remodel, 1,500 sq. ft.

602/604/612 Colorado Mixed-Use Building, Santa Monica, 1989
Renovation for galleries, nonprofit agency offices, womens' shelter, and homeless drop-in center, 33,000 sq. ft.

Commercial

Digital Domain, Venice, 1994; interior improvements providing offices, computer graphics area, screening room, art department, and movie stages, 67,000 sq. ft.

Lightstorm Entertainment, Santa Monica, 1993; interior improvements providing production offices and THX theater, 33,000 sq. ft.

Gilmore Bank, Los Angeles, 1995; remodel and modernization of bank, 12,000 sq. ft.

Gilmore Bank Office Building, Los Angeles, 1992 (design through construction documentation), 25,000 sq. ft.

1548–1550 Studios, Santa Monica, 1989 and 1994; tenant improvements, 5,400 sq. ft.

Retail

Grandma's Kitchen, Los Angeles, 1996; fast-food facility renovation

Farmers Market, Los Angeles, 1992; addition to retail complex; master plan, landscape/parking plan, and exterior improvements; wine bar, coffee store, fruit stand, salad stand, and other tenant improvements, 70,000 sq. ft.

Stage Deli, Los Angeles, 1987; deli and restaurant, 7,600 sq. ft.

Century City Food Hall, Los Angeles, 1987; tenant review architects

Multiunit Housing

5th Street Family Housing, Santa Monica, 1997 (estimated completion), 32 units of affordable family apartments

Boyd Hotel, Los Angeles, 1996; 63-room single room occupancy hotel

Simone Hotel, Los Angeles, 1992; 122-room single room occupancy hotel

Given Triplex, Santa Monica, 1992; three 1,500 sq. ft. condominiums

Electric ArtBlock (with Glenn D. Erikson, AIA), Venice, 1988; 20 units of new artist loft housing

St. John's Hospital Replacement Housing, Santa Monica, 1989. A total of 24 affordable apartments on 3 sites
Berkeley Street, 7 units; 18th Street, 6 units; Arizona Avenue, 11 units

Ozone Beach Boxes, Venice, 1989; 6-unit condominium project

Liffman House, Santa Monica, 1988; 6-unit congregate seniors' housing for Alternative Living for the Aging (non profit agency)

Millen Apartments, Santa Monica, 1988; 3 units

Community Corp. of Santa Monica Housing, Santa Monica, 1987
OP12, two 6-unit affordable apartment developments; Cloverfield Project, 62-unit rehabilitation project; Modular Housing, three 6-unit affordable apartment developments

Hollywood Duplex, Hollywood Hills, 1987; 2 units

17th Street Addition, Santa Monica, 1985; renovation/addition to 6-unit apartment building

California Avenue Duplex, Santa Monica, 1982; 2 units

Single-Family Houses

Evans Road House, Pacific Palisades, 1997; new house

Hawaii House, Waimea, Hawaii, 1996; new house

Zabin House, Santa Monica, 1995; new house

Schaap/Quinlin Remodel, Santa Monica, 1995; residential earthquake repair and remodel

Erenberg House, Santa Monica, 1995; remodel/addition

Pelcyger House, Los Angeles, 1994; remodel/addition

31st Street House, Santa Monica, 1993; remodel/addition
Farenga House, Los Angeles, 1993; remodel/second-floor addition
Tarzana House, Tarzana, 1992; new house
Georgina House, Santa Monica, 1991; remodel/second-floor addition
Kerr House, Culver City, 1991; remodel
Woelfle/Erskin House, Venice, 1990; remodel/addition
Koning Eizenberg House, Santa Monica, 1989; new house
Maple Street House, Santa Monica, 1989; remodel/second-floor addition
Moore's Folly, Malibu, 1989; addition
Molloy House, Los Angeles, 1988; remodel/addition
Mandeville Canyon House, Los Angeles, 1987; remodel
Wendel Franzen House, Santa Monica, 1986; remodel/addition
Given-Dennis House, Santa Monica, 1984; remodel/addition
Rosen House, Mar Vista, 1984; home office addition

Artists' Studios
Cheng & Chu Studios, Santa Monica, 1990
Karla Klarin Studio, Santa Monica, 1987
McMillen Studio, Santa Monica, 1984

Urban Design
MTA Metro Station Master Plan, Los Angeles, 1993
Master plan study for transit-based housing around the Santa Monica Blvd. and Vermont Ave. Metro Station area for the LA Metropolitan Transportation Authority
Vitalize Fairfax Project, Los Angeles, 1984; streetscape and storefront improvement program

Competition Entries

Museum of Victoria, Melbourne, Australia, 1994
West Hollywood Civic Center, West Hollywood, 1987
St. Paul Cityscape Design Competition (with Michael McMillen), St. Paul, Minnesota, 1985
The Peak (with William J. Mitchell and Tom Kvan), Hong Kong, 1982; private club

Exhibitions

"WWW [world wide work]: An Exhibition of Global Architecture by Fax," Curve Architecture, Australia, June 1995
"Currents," Harvard University Graduate School of Design, September 1994
"House Rules" Wexner Center for the Arts, Columbus, Ohio, August 1994
"The Architect's Dream: Houses for the Next Millennium," Contemporary Arts Center, Cincinnati, Ohio, November 1993
"Angels & Franciscans: Innovative Architecture from Los Angeles and San Francisco," Leo Castelli/Gagosian Gallery, New York, September 1992; Santa Monica Museum of Art, Santa Monica, California, February 1993
"Broadening the Discourse," exhibit and conference, California Women in Environmental Design, February 1992
Exhibition of Koning Eizenberg projects, Graduate School of Architecture and Urban Planning, University of California at Los Angeles, Fall 1990
"The Socially Responsible Environment: USA/USSR 1980–1990," Architects, Designers and Planners for Social Responsibility, traveling exhibition, November 1990
"Architects' Furniture," Gallery of Functional Art, Los Angeles, January 1990
Young Architects Exhibition, School of Architecture, University of Technology Sydney, Australia, September 1988
"Reweaving the Urban Fabric: International Approaches to Infill Housing," curated by the New York State Council on the Arts and the New York Landmarks Conservancy, PaineWebber Gallery, New York, March 1988

Awards

1996	National Concrete/Masonry Award – Sepulveda Gymnasium
	Honor Award, AIA California Council – Sepulveda Gymnasium
	National AIA Honor Award for Architecture – 31st Street House
1995	Design Award, AIA San Fernando Valley Chapter – Sepulveda Gymnasium
	Record House Award (*Architectural Record*) – 31st Street House
1994	National AIA Honor Award for Architecture – Simone Hotel
	Honor Award, AIA California Council – 31st Street House
1993–94	Sunset Western Home Awards Citation – Tarzana House
1993	Los Angeles Business Council Beautification Award, Mixed-Use Commercial/Residential – Electric ArtBlock
	Los Angeles Business Council Award Finalist, Low-Income Housing – Simone Hotel
1992	Award of Merit, AIA Los Angeles Chapter – Tarzana House
1991	Westside Urban Forum Prize, Real Estate Development-Land Use Planning/Urban Design - Farmers Market Historic Preservation
	Award of Merit, AIA Los Angeles Chapter – Koning Eizenberg House
	Los Angeles Business Council Beautification Award Finalist, Public Use/Civic Project – Ken Edwards Center for Community Services
1989	Domino's Top 30 Architects
1988	Record House Award (*Architectural Record*) – Hollywood Duplex
1987	First Award, 34th Annual P/A Awards (*Progressive Architecture*), Affordable Housing – OP12 Berkeley Street Housing

Bibliography

1996   De Vido, Alfredo. *House Design: Art + Practice* (New York: John Wiley & Sons, 1996), pp. 92–93.
Hellman, Peter. "Housing with Heart," *Metropolitan Home*, March–April 1996 (Simone Hotel).
Stein, Karen D. "Bank Job," *Architectural Record,* February 1996, pp. 72–75.

1995   "Current Exhibitions: Koning Eizenberg Architecture 31st Street House," *GSD News*, Harvard University Graduate School of Design, Winter/Spring 1995, p. 43.
Davis, Sam. *The Architecture of Affordable Housing* (Berkeley and Los Angeles: The University of California Press, 1995), pp. 169–78.
Dixon, John Morris. "The Santa Monica School: What's Its Lasting Contribution?" *Progressive Architecture,* May 1995, pp. 63–71, 112.
Gallery MA. *581 Architects in the World* (Tokyo: Gallery MA, 1995), p. 367.
Stein, Karen D. "Family Matters," *Architectural Record,* Record Houses issue, April 1995, pp. 88–91.

1994   "31st Street House," *Architecture Now* (Mulgrave, Australia: The Images Publishing Group, 1994), pp 9.1–9.14.
"House Rules Project: Koning Eizenberg Architecture and bell hooks," *l'ARCA* 85 (September 1994): 79.
"Los Angeles: Urban Landscape & Architecture," *Abitare*, May 1994, pp. 142, 174–75.
"Simone Hotel in Los Angeles, United States," *AW* 160 (December 1994): 14–15.
De Michelis, Marco. "Combinatory Exercises On The Work of Koning Eizenberg in Los Angeles," *Casabella,* May 1994, pp. 58–66, 71.

Forgey, Benjamin. "Beyond Beauty: Structures that Serve," *The Washington Post*, February 5, 1994, Style section, p. G1.

Gebhard, David, and Robert Winter. *Los Angeles: An Architectural Guide* (Layton, Utah: Gibbs-Smith Publishers, 1994).

Giovannini, Joseph. "A Masterpiece of Modesty," *Metropolitan Home*, September/October 1994, pp. 90–95.

———. "L.A. Architects: They Did It Their Way," *Los Angeles Times Magazine*, May 15, 1994, pp. 30–37.

Gregory, Daniel. "A Wall For All Reasons," *Sunset*, January 1994, p. 88.

hooks, bell; Julie Eizenberg and Hank Koning. "House, 20 June 1994," *Assemblage* 24 (August 1994): 22–29.

Muschamp, Herbert. "Ten Little Houses and How They Grew," *The New York Times*, October 16, 1994, Arts & Leisure section 2, p. 40.

Sutro, Dirk. *West Coast Wave: New California Houses* (New York: Van Nostrand Reinhold, 1994), pp. 101–105.

Varady, Stephen. "Santa Monica Suburbia," *Architecture Australia,* July/August 1994, pp. 44–49.

Webb, Michael. "Architecture: Homes of Their Own," *Los Angeles Times Magazine,* November 27, 1994, pp. 44–48, 56.

———. *Architects House Themselves.* (Washington, D.C.: The Preservation Press [National Trust for Historic Preservation], 1994), pp. 110–13.

———. *Architects' Guide to Los Angeles* (Los Angeles: American Institute of Architects/Los Angeles Chapter, 1994).

Yagi, Koji. *Transformation of American Houses* (Tokyo: Tokyo Institute of Technology, 1994).

1993

"AIA/LA Design Awards 1992: Tarzana House," *L.A. Architect,* December 1992/January 1993, p. 14.

"American Dream," RAUM & WOHNEN, January/February 1993, pp. 42–43.

"The 40th Annual P/A Awards," *Progressive Architecture,* January 1993, pp. 41–93.

Barrett, Roger. "Koning Eizenberg," *Architecture Australia,* May-June 1993, pp. 30–35.

Gregory, Daniel. "Every Story Frames a Picture: 1993–1994 Western Home Awards," *Sunset,* October 1993, pp. 92–93.

Larson, Magali. *Behind the Post-Modern Facade* (Berkeley and Los Angeles: The University of California Press, 1993).

Le Blanc, Sydney. *The Whitney Guide to Twentieth-Century American Architecture* (New York: The Whitney Library of Design, 1993).

Pittel, Christine, and Elizabeth Sverbeyeff Byron. "A Tree House in Tarzana," *Elle Decor,* December 1992/January 1993, pp. 70–77.

Ryan, Raymund. "California Commune," *Architectural Review,* June 1993, pp. 59–62.

Sheine, Judith. "Housing California: Skid Row Star," *Architecture,* January 1993, pp. 43–47.

———. "Vermont/Santa Monica Station Metro Rail Red Line," and "Los Angeles Builds on Transportation," *Architecture,* August 1993, pp. 93–99.

1992

Anderton, Frances. "Buildings in Venice," *L.A. Architect,* May 1992, pp. 8–11.

Betsky, Aaron. "Ken Edwards Center Shapes Up to Be a User-Friendly Building," *Los Angeles Times,* Westside Digest, January 16, 1992, p. J2.

Fujii, Wayne. "Santa Monica Residence," *GA HOUSES 33* (February 1992): 150–59.

Ishiguro, Tomoko. "Architectural Concepts for the Elders," *AXIS,* Winter 1992, p. 16.

Lacy, Bill, and Susan deMenil, eds. *Angels & Franciscans: Innovative Architecture from Los Angeles and San Francisco* (New York: Rizzoli International Publications and Leo Castelli/Gagosian Gallery, 1992).

Muschamp, Herbert. "The Genius of California Visits SoHo," *The New York Times,* Weekend Section, October 2, 1992, pp. C1 and C29.

Newman, Morris. "Site Strategies: Life (and Work) in Venice," *Progressive Architecture,* August 1992, pp. 52–55.

Webb, Michael. "Koning Eizenberg Architecture," *Interior Architecture 37* (1992): 112–19.

1991

Betsky, Aaron, et al. *Experimental Architecture in Los Angeles* (New York: Rizzoli International Publications, 1991), pp. 90–95.

Branch, Mark Alden. "Affordable Housing: Projects, San Julian Single Room Occupancy Hotel," *Progressive Architecture,* June 1991, p. 104.

Davis, Carl. "Housing for Artists?" *L.A. Architect,* February 1991, pp. 4–5, 10.

Ghirardo, Diane. "El Juego de las Piezas," *A & V 32* (1991): 19–20, 46–48.

Hay, David. "Designs on LA," *HQ Magazine* (New Zealand), April 1991, pp. 104–109.

Komaki, Satoru. "Tarzana House," *GA HOUSES 31* (April 1991): 106–107.

Lievre, Veronique. "From Drawing Board to Drawing Room," *Angeles*, February 1991, pp. 31–33.

Mann, Lian Hurst. "Women on the Rise," *L.A. Architect,* October 1991.

Mitchell, Mary. "AIA/LA Design Awards 1991: 909 House," *L.A. Architect,* December 1991, p. 6.

Nesmith, Lynn. "Coming of Age," *Architecture,* March 1991, pp. 98–103.

Newman, Morris. "20 Loft-Studios for Artists," *The New York Times,* May 12, 1991, Real Estate Section.

———. "An Accidental City: Abbot Kinney, A Part of Venice That is About to Go," *Design LA,* October 1991, pp. 22–23.

Tanaka, Ken. "California Avenue Duplex," *World Residential Design* 01 (Tokyo: N.I.C. Ltd., The Moriyama Editors Studio, 1991).

1990

"La Casa Canyon," *Abitare,* April 1990, pp. 140–47.

Ghirardo, Diane. "Low Cost Houses und CRA," *Werk Bauen & Wohnen,* July 8, 1990, pp. 58–61.

Iovine, Julie V. "Blueprint for the New Family Home," *Metropolitan Home,* December 1990, pp. 112–19.

Lang, Werner. "Neues aus L.A." *Baumeister,* October 1990, p. 40.

McGregor, Alexander. "Home in their Range," *Melbourne Sunday Herald,* March 4, 1990, pp. 44–47.

Mulard, Claudine. "Enclave Californienne," *Archi-Cree,* February 1990, pp. 90–95.

Paine, A. "Crystalline LA," *Architectural Review,* April 1990, pp. 94–96.

Sato, Toshiro. "Women in Architecture," *SD,* June 1990, pp. 10–11.

Webb, Michael. "Into the Garden," *Architecture,* March 1990, pp. 136–41.

———. "Long on Design," *L.A. Style,* February 1990, pp. 110–13.

Yamashita, Arika. "California New Wave," *AT Architecture Magazine,* December 1990, pp. 25–27.

1989

Betsky, Aaron. "Steel Chick and Stucco Dreams at the L.A. Lab," *Metropolitan Home,* August 1989, pp. 75–87.

Ghirardo, Diane. "Faces/Architecture," *ELLE,* June 1989, p. 42.

Szenasy, S. "Making Home Work," *Metropolis,* March 1989, pp. 60–65, 85–86.

Webb, Michael. "California Scheming," *BELLE,* October-November 1989, pp. 34–37.

———. "Lofts in Suburbia," *Los Angeles Times Magazine,* August 6, 1989, pp. 30–31.

1988

"88 for 1988: Hank Koning and Julie Eizenberg, Architects," *Los Angeles Times Magazine,* January 10, 1988, p. 7.

"Hollywood Duplex," *Nikkei Architecture,* October 1988, pp. 217–19.

"Koning Eizenberg Architecture," *GA HOUSES* 24 (October 1988): 46–155.

Bartle, Andrew, and Jonathan Kirschenfeld. "The Big Country," *Ottagono,* September 1988, pp. 20–45, reference pg. 30.

Brenner, Douglas. "Double Feature: Hollywood Duplex," *Architectural Record,* Record Houses issue, mid-April 1988, pp. 90–95.

C.I.A. News, Spring 1988 (Tokyo: Creative Intelligence Associates, Inc.), pp. 3, 11.

Clagett, Leslie. "Material Cultured," *Home,* May 1988, p. 92.

Freiman, Ziva. "New Voices in Architecture: Celebrating the Basics," *Metropolitan Home,* February 1988, pp. 86–87.

Goldberger, Paul. "Fashions in Bricks and Mortar Make Room for Conscience," *The New York Times,* December 25, 1988.

Gordon, Alice. "Talking to…Mildred Friedman," *Vogue,* April 1988, pp. 204, 208, 214.

Langdon, Philip. "HOME: Where Sprawl Comes to Squeeze: Solving New Problems of Density in LA," *The Atlantic,* January 1988, pp. 85–88.

Leavitt, Jacqueline. "Low-Cost Housing," *Progressive Architecture,* October 1988, pp. 70–75.

Reed, Rochelle. "Interiors: Irreverent Renovation," *Los Angeles Times Magazine,* April 3, 1988, pp. 34–35.

Swenarton, Mark. "Housing: Rates of Exchange," *Building Design,* October 14, 1988, pp. 20–23.

Widom, Chester A. "Shared Housing," *Architecture California,* July/August 1988, pp. 28–29.

1987

"Alumni Profiles: Hank Koning and Julie Eizenberg, Progressive Architecture First Award," *UCLA Architecture and Planning,* Fall 1987, p. 22.

"Design News," *Architectural Record,* November 1987, p. 67.

"Hank Koning and Julie Eizenberg: Houses, Hollywood Hills," *Architectural Review,* December 1987, pp. 48/12–49/12.

"The 34th Annual P/A Awards," *Progressive Architecture,* January 1987 (First Award: Affordable Housing).

Favro, Diane. "Women in Architecture: The Julia Morgan Colloquium," *UCLA Architecture & Planning,* Fall 1987, pp. 17–19.

Kaplan, Sam Hall. "A Tour of Eclectic L.A. Architecture," *Los Angeles Times,* March 14, 1987, Part V, pp. 1 and 5.

———. "L.A. Architects Score Impressively," *Los Angeles Times,* February 22, 1987, Real Estate Section, p. 2.

Whiteson, Leon. "Down Under Architects Find Themselves on Top," *Los Angeles Herald Examiner,* February 22, 1987, p. E9.

1986

"A Home Office by the Drive..." *Sunset,* February 1986, p. 130.

"Step by Step: An Invisible Trellis," *Home,* July 1986, pp. 72–73.

Ravid, Joyce. "The Met Grill: A Conversation with Architect Richard Meier," *Metropolitan Home,* September 1986, pp. 24, 111–13.

Rieselbach, Anne. "California Collage," *House and Garden,* January 1986, pp. 26–27.

Street-Porter, Tim. *Freestyle: The New Architecture & Design from Los Angeles* (New York: Stewart, Tabori & Chang, 1986), pp. 215–17.

Viladas, Pilar. "Style and Substance: A Portfolio of Built Work by Koning Eizenberg," *Progressive Architecture,* February 1986, pp. 110–15.

1981–1985

"Downsizing the American Dream," *UCLA Architecture and Planning*, Winter 1983, p. 25.

"Koning Eizenberg Kvan Mitchell: The Peak, Hong Kong," *UCLA Architecture and Planning,* Alumni Architecture issue, Summer 1984, p. 25.

"Shove the Bed Away from the Wall," *Sunset,* November 1985, pp. 194–95.

Eizenberg, Julie, and Hank Koning. "The Language of the Prairie: Frank Lloyd Wright's Prairie Houses," *Environment and Planning B,* vol. 8 (October 1981): 295–323.

The Home (New York: MacMillan, 1985), pp. 74, 100, 104, 111, 122, 160–61.

Illustration Credits

William Abranowicz 185 right, 190

Roland Bishop 78

Ron Forth 213

Courtesy of Gilmore Bank 50, 55 upper

Tim Griffith cover, 180, 182, 184, 185 left, 186–189, 191–193

© David Hewitt / Anne Garrison 34–37, 39 right, 41

Richard K. Loesch 217

© Grant Mudford 20, 22, 25–27, 29–30, 32, 48, 51–54, 55 lower, 56, 64–75, 156, 157 lower, 160, 165 upper right, lower left

Jan Paul Pletrzak 38, 39 left; 42, 79–87, 89

© Tim Street-Porter 90–92, 94 lower, 95 lower, 96–101,104–105, 108 (courtesy of Esto), 111–119, 121–125, 130–133, 136–141, 154 (courtesy of *Metropolitan Home* magazine, Hachette Filipacchi USA Inc.),162, 163,164 upper left, lower left and right, 165 upper left, lower right, 170, 173, 175–179, 194–197, 200–206, back cover

Tradecraft Studios / Steven L. Gardner 127

Dominique Vorillon 157 upper, 164 upper right

© Koning Eizenberg Architecture all other drawings and photographs

What Would Your Dream House Be? was commissioned by The Contemporary Arts Center in Cincinnati, Ohio, for the exhibition "The Architect's Dream: Houses for the Next Millenium" in 1993.

House, 20 June 1994 was commissioned by the Wexner Center for the Arts at The Ohio State University in Columbus, Ohio, for the exhibition "House Rules" in 1994.

Julie Eizenberg

Julie Eizenberg attended the School of Architecture at the University of Melbourne from 1972 to 1977. She worked for Public Works Department of Victoria, Peter Jones Landscape Architect, and Jackson & Walker Architects until traveling to the U.S. in 1979 to pursue a Master of Architecture at the University of California at Los Angeles. In 1981, together with Hank Koning, Julie Eizenberg established an architectural practice in Santa Monica. Eizenberg is licensed as an architect in Victoria, Australia, and the U.S. and is currently an Associate Adjunct Professor at UCLA. She has also taught at MIT and the Harvard University Graduate School of Design, among other schools, and lectured extensively in the U.S. and abroad.

Hank Koning, FAIA, FRAIA

Hank Koning attended the School of Architecture at the University of Melbourne from 1972 to 1977. He worked first for Hank Romyn, Architect, and then Max May, Architect Pty. Ltd., until traveling to the U.S. in 1979 to pursue a Master of Architecture at the University of California at Los Angeles. In 1981, together with Julie Eizenberg, Hank Koning established an architectural practice in Santa Monica. He is licensed as an architect in Australia and the U.S. and is a Fellow of both the American Institute of Architects and the Royal Australian Institute of Architects. Koning maintains an interest in pedagogical issues and has lectured and taught at many institutions both in the U.S. and abroad, including UCLA, the Harvard University Graduate School of Design, the University of British Columbia, and the University of Hong Kong.

Employees and Interns

Tim Andreas
Hector Ayala
Nathaniel Bach
Fernando Bracer
Andy Bristol
J. Michael Brown
Alex Bushkoff
Gustave Carlson
Rogerio Carvalheiro
Michael Ching
John Davis
Konrad Deffner
Jay Deguchi
John Echlin
Sarah Elzas
Stuart Emmons
Tom Goffigon
Yo-ichiro Hakomori
Chris Hendricks
Timothy Horton
Leem-jong Jang
Tom Jin
Eric Kaiser
Kim Karcher
Florian Kastle
Robin Kremen
Brian Lane
Kim Lavacot
Elizabeth Lenel
David Light
Dion McCarthy
Alberto Mendoza
Mernoosh Mojalloli
Michael Murray
Domingo Ottolia
Neil Peoples
Angelo San Diego
Marc Schoeplein
James Simeo
Jennifer Spangler
Susan Stevens
Elaine Sun
Kevin Tyrrell
Peter Vogel
Dorothea Voitlander
Dason Whitsett
Brad Williams
Heidi Williams
Kristen Wogen
David Woo
Marla Woodhouse